A 1950s Mother

Other Books by Sheila Hardy

The Village School, Boydell Press/Anglia TV, 1979

1804 …That was the Year …, Brechinset, 1986

The Story of Anne Candler, SPA, 1988

The Diary of a Suffolk Farmer's Wife: 1854–69,
Macmillan, 1992

Treason's Flame, Square One Publishing, 1995

Tattingstone: A Village and Its People, self-published, 2000

*The House on the Hill: The Samford House of Industry
1764–1930*, self-published, 2001

*An Admirable Wife: The Life and Times of Frances,
Lady Nelson*, Spellmount, 2005

The Cretingham Murder, The History Press, 2008

Arsenic in the Dumplings: A Casebook of Suffolk Poisonings,
The History Press, 2010

The Real Mrs Beeton: The Story of Eliza Acton,
The History Press, 2011

Murder and Crime in Suffolk, The History Press, 2012

A 1950s Housewife, The HistoryPress, 2012

A 1950s Mother

Bringing up Baby in the 1950s

Sheila Hardy

To the memory of Frances Hutchinson, the mother
who laid the foundations of my life.

First published 2013
This paperback edition published 2022

The History Press
97 St George's Place, Cheltenham,
Gloucestershire, GL50 3QB
www.thehistorypress.co.uk

British Library Cataloguing in Publication Data.
A catalogue record for this book is available from the British Library.

ISBN 978 0 7509 9934 2

Typesetting and origination by The History Press
Printed and bound in Great Britain by TJ Books Limited, Padstow, Cornwall.

MIX
Paper from
responsible sources
FSC® C013056

Trees for Life

Contents

Acknowledgements

*E*very time I embark on the long journey to produce a book, I am amazed by the kindness often of complete strangers who are willing to share with me either their expertise on a subject or their personal experiences. Never has the latter been put more to the test than in this case and in the making of its predecessor, *A 1950s Housewife*. Many women, now in their seventies and eighties, generously revealed personal details of their lives in answers to my questionnaires; some allowed me to attend their group meetings where exchanges of information often sparked off hitherto little known facts. To the following ladies whom I call my '1950s Mothers' my debt of gratitude is enormous. To those who permitted me to use their stories to illustrate certain aspects, I hope they feel I have done them justice. So, thank you to: Mesdames Angland, Billsberry, Bland, Bolton, Brittain, Coker,

Cox, Jacobs, Lankester, Lawrence, Lemon, Perrins, Porter, Randall, Richardson, Slater, Smith, Stannard, Watkins and Williams.

When talking to the members of the Chantry Library 55 Alive group I hit an extra vein of gold with the discovery that some of them were '1950s children'. They too were most helpful with their recollections of their earliest memories as well as being able to provide some interesting photographs. Friends and relations were also dragooned into looking back; included in this group of 'children' are: Pauline Atkins, Diane Bell, A. Best, Helen Best, D. Bray, Mary Bray, Susan Garrod, Tony Garrod, Guy Smith, the Sullivan family, Colleen Taylor and Steve Williams. Mrs Pamela Green freely gave of her time to write in much detail of her experiences as a teacher in the 1950s and the Rt Rev John Waine, former bishop of St Edmundsbury and Ipswich, answered my questions concerning the service of Churching of Women, while Rachel Field helped with some background research. The following three people played a vital part by providing me with valuable printed material; so a very special thank you to Ursula Hardy for the loan of books used in her training as a Norland nanny, a precious copy of *Woman's Weekly* and various knitting patterns. Valerie Clift lent me some rare copies of *Mother and Baby* magazines from the 1950s and John Kirkland allowed me to draw freely upon the *Stitchcraft* magazines collected by his late wife, Monica. To each and every one of you a most inadequate thank you; without your contribution, this book could not have been written. And finally, a huge thank you to Sophie Bradshaw for giving me the challenge and making me accept that the 1950s are now considered history!

Introduction

It seems to be almost too good to be true that the middle decade of the twentieth century, that is 1955, should have been the divide between the old order and the new. So many of the accepted customs and taboos of previous centuries were broken down or swept away as 'modern' ideas and methods took their place. While younger people readily took to the new ways, older people clung to what they considered were the best, whether in fashion or food, grammar schools or comprehensives. The clash between the old ways and the new thinking was likely to show itself most strongly where child rearing was concerned, especially if mothers were much in evidence to influence their daughters and daughters-in-law when the young women became pregnant. In a previous book, *A 1950s Housewife*, we met a group of women who volunteered their personal experiences of married life in that decade. In this volume, they and others reveal something of the advice and problems they encountered in bringing up their babies. The one thing that a young mother never lacked was being told how she should manage her child. The debate on the 'correct' way to rear a child continues today, just as it has done from time immemorial.

The most illustrious mother of the 1950s was HRH Princess Elizabeth who already had two small children when she became queen following the death of her father King George VI in 1952. The two young princesses, Elizabeth and Margaret Rose had had the benefit of growing up in a loving family, enjoying a very close relationship with their parents, quite unlike the rigid, regimented childhood the king and his siblings had known. However, the very nature of their position in society meant that royal children would be raised in entirely different circumstances from the mainstream population; their day-to-day care would fall to nannies and nursemaids, and contact with their parents would be limited. Whereas the norm for the general population at that time was for the child to spend most of its early years in close proximity to its mother who looked after its needs, while its father provided for them all by working and thus was a more remote figure in the child's life.

The difference between the family life experienced by our present queen and that of her father exemplifies some of the attitudes to bringing up children that seem to have existed since civilization began. Such guidance as parents were given in the past rested on the belief that children should not be left to develop freely but, like young animals, they needed to be taught or trained how to do the right thing. How that training was to be achieved was pretty straight forward. The

Bible tells us in Proverbs XIII, v.24, that training should be given with love; albeit a love that on occasions has been misinterpreted: 'He that spares the rod hates his son but he that loves him chastens him betimes.' That is, the parent who neglects to correct his child really does not care about the child at all the loving parent punishes wrongdoing when necessary. In a later chapter, Proverbs XXII, v.6, we are told: 'Train up a child in the way he should go: and when he is old, he will not depart from it.'

Similar ideas occur in the work of the sixth-century Chinese teacher Yan Zhitui, who gave clear instructions on how a baby should be raised:

> ... as soon as a lovely baby can recognize facial expressions and understand approval and disapproval, training should be begun so that he would do what he is told to do and stop when ordered. After a few years of this, punishment with the bamboo can be minimised, as parental strictness and dignity mingled with parental love will lead boys and girls to a feeling of respect and caution and give rise to filial piety ...
>
> Wherever there is love without training this result is never achieved. Children eat, drink, speak and act as they please. Instead of needing prohibitions, they receive praise, instead of urgent reprimands they receive smiles. Even when children are old enough to learn, such treatment is still regarded the proper method. Only after the child has formed proud and arrogant habits do they try to control him. But one may whip a child to death and he will not be respectful, while the growing anger of the parents only increases his resentment. After he grows up such a child at last becomes nothing but a scoundrel.
>
> *The Family Instructions of Master Yan*

From such sources grew the idea that discipline by some form of corporal punishment went hand-in-hand with training. Hence the continued belief in 'spare the rod and spoil the child'. Poet Thomas Hood, in his 'The Irish Schoolmaster', wrote: 'He never spoils the child and spares the rod, But spoils the rod and never spares the child.' By the time we reach the Victorian age, the rod is still much in evidence both at home and in the schoolroom, and for girls as well as boys. In extreme cases the idea of loving training seems to have been lost and with it all forms of affection. The nineteenth century abounds with literary examples of those children who were either not correctly trained or were over-indulged by their mothers, growing up to become unprincipled and selfish adults. In contrast some authors depicted the over-disciplined children as growing into unhappy adults incapable of either giving or receiving love. That oft-quoted axiom 'children should be seen and not heard' was one that lingered long in certain aspects of the British way of life. In the 1950s, children were expected to be well mannered, sit quietly largely ignored, when taken to visit friends and relations, and were told quite firmly never to interrupt the adults' conversation.

The end of the nineteenth century found Britain with an ever-increasing population, much of which was living in poor, overcrowded housing lacking running water and adequate sewage disposal. Insufficient food and generally poor nutrition often led to disease and physical impairments, which sentenced a child to a life either as a permanent invalid in a squalid home, or as a long-term inmate of the workhouse. Without proper methods of birth control families increased alarmingly, eased only by a high mortality rate among babies. The lack of proper medical care often resulted in the death of women following childbirth, which in turn led to a family of orphans left either to shift for themselves as best they could or having to be placed in an orphanage.

At a time when the only State assistance for the poor came from the Poor Law, which was paid for by the Parish Poor Rate, it fell to charitable organisations, often inspired by religious zeal, to do what they could to help alleviate the suffering of those most in need. Among them were campaigners and practical workers like Dr Barnado, who worked to rescue children found living on the streets, and William Booth, who formed his Salvation Army to battle for those addicted to drink in the hope that, by saving them, whole families would be rescued from destitution. He also provided practical and lasting help by establishing hospitals for the poor in major cities. Bands of Evangelical Christian women worked tirelessly to provide food and clothing for poor families in their local areas, some volunteering to teach children in Ragged Schools in an effort to use education as a way of providing the rising generation with the ability to find employment.

In some of the most impoverished areas of London and other cities, wealthy middle-class women who were members of the High Anglican Church came together to form sisterhoods, their convents offering shelter and work, in particular for 'fallen women'. For many young girls, forced out of overcrowded homes, prostitution was often the only way they could earn enough to feed themselves and pay for shelter. Inevitably, these girls, some as young as 13 and 14, became pregnant. Without family or friends to fall back on, they were reduced to abject poverty, open to becoming the prey of dissolute rogues who forced them into stealing or prostitution, usually both. These were the 'fallen' the sisters tried to help. Chafing at a life of indolence and indulgence, many of the middle- and upper-class women who joined the sisterhoods were thwarted nurses. Prompted by their religious faith they had the desire to minister to the poor in this way, but although their parents and guardians might countenance a bit of 'do-gooding' on their daughters' behalf one or two afternoons a week, and while it was allowable for them to visit the sick with a basket containing a jar of beef tea or a nourishing soup, it was quite a different matter for them to want to go off and become a trained nurse. The idea was abhorrent, for even though the number of hospitals throughout the country was increasing, nurses at that time were not drawn from the middle classes. Those women who rebelled and joined the sisterhoods often had to go to the continent to get the training they needed, and before long they were taking their expertise into hospitals and supervising other nurses. Their contribution is still remembered today, having given their title to the senior nurse in a hospital ward.

Since it was considered a natural procedure until the eighteenth century, women gave birth in their own homes assisted by other women, those who had had children themselves and more often those who had, with much practice, become self-appointed midwives. Only in dire emergencies was a medical practitioner called in to assist at the actual birth. When the earliest union workhouses were set up in the eighteenth century they included an infirmary to treat seriously ill inmates, which also oversaw the care of pregnant and nursing mothers. The period immediately following a birth was known as 'the lying-in' and this was the title adopted for the first maternity hospitals set up in London. Significantly, the very first, established in

1749, was known as 'The lying-in hospital for Married Women'. The unmarried mother, as we know from Charles Dickens and Thomas Hardy, had to seek her lying-in in the workhouse. The Lying-In Hospitals took their patients for three weeks, beginning a week before they were due to be delivered. They were, of course, fee-paying, apart from exceptional cases. Initially, they were quite small establishments but they served as ideal training ground for the specialist nurses who became midwives. By the twentieth century midwives were in great demand and by the time we get to the 1950s, as we shall see in the pages that follow, every expectant mother was automatically assigned to the care of a midwife.

Quite apart from any help and advice on childcare that doctors and midwives might provide on a personal level, the twentieth century inspired other medical professionals to write about their experiences and the methods they had used in the rearing of babies and young people. The most influential of these was the New Zealander Dr (later Sir) Frederick Truby King (1858–1938). He spent much of his working life as the superintendent of a mental institution, where his research led him to the conclusion that mental ill health was the result of a faulty up-bringing. His regime of a good diet, fresh air, exercise, work, recreation and rest for his patients appeared to achieve good results. When he turned his attention to young children, he came to the conclusion that the cow's milk on which babies were fed was responsible for many of their ills, and having been impressed during a visit to Japan on the health of the infants there, where breast-feeding was the norm, he proposed that this should be the basis of good child-rearing. He published *Feeding and Care of Baby* in 1913. Thereafter the book became both widely read and adopted throughout the world. Most of the women who became mothers in the 1950s would have been brought up on the general precepts laid down by King, whose work was carried on enthusiastically in this country by Mabel Liddiard.

So it was that our expectant mothers and fathers, too, would be reading books and magazine articles that would offer advice that had been tried and tested for forty years. However much the magazines of the day attempted to reflect modern ideas, they still tended to echo the old views and it would take time before those of the American Dr Spock would revolutionise the thinking of the 1960s.

Note

In the 1950s the word 'gender' was most likely to have been used in classrooms to teach pupils learning Latin, French and German how to distinguish the correct ending to apply to a noun. It was a somewhat difficult concept for the average English child to comprehend that one's eye, ear, nose and mouth, for example, might be labelled masculine, feminine or neuter, and to make matters worse, a feminine noun in one language might well be masculine or neuter in another. The words 'sexist' and 'feminism' were to enter the vocabulary of some during the 1960s. I mention this to explain why I have adopted the use throughout of 'he' when describing babies of both sexes. To write he/she is both time wasting and seems clumsy while 'it' seems disrespectful. There are books where the author has deliberately written of the baby throughout as female; to me, that seems slightly forced. Belonging to a generation even earlier than the 1950s, I happily accepted the idea that 'he' stood for *all* humankind.

1

Expecting

*T*he words 'pregnancy' and 'pregnant' were not in general use amongst the majority of the population in the early 1950s. Instead, a woman was described, even on official forms, as an expectant mother, while her friends and relations all busily reported that she was 'expecting'. The word pregnant had been in popular use in the eighteenth and early nineteenth century but fell into obscurity during the Victorian era, possibly because the condition was not considered one to be discussed in general conversation. A young scholar of the 1950s was more likely to come across the word 'pregnant' only in its literary context of describing a dramatic pause.

Most of those who have contributed their memories became pregnant within eighteen months to two and a half years after marriage. Some of them were still limited to living in two rooms in someone else's home and having to share the kitchen and bathroom. For others, the advent of a baby meant that they were able to progress a bit further up the waiting list for a council house. Certainly the incentive to have a proper home of their own became stronger once the realisation struck of what having a baby would entail.

In those days before pregnancy-testing kits, most women waited until a second period was missed before visiting their doctor to have their suspicions confirmed. Once he, and most doctors at that time were men, had examined her thoroughly and given her a date for her confinement, he then directed her to the antenatal clinic to make arrangements for where the birth should take place. The doctor also provided her with the necessary certificate to take or send to the local Pensions and National Insurance Office, which would ensure that she was provided with the extra care given by the State. During the war years of the 1940s, when rationing was introduced to ensure fair shares of food supplies for all, there was, according to Nurse Patterson who gave expert advice in a magazine, 'a universal improvement in children's health. Britain's Bonny Babies became a by-word. Expectant mothers had the first call on the nation's larder and priority for milk.' One result of the doctor's certificate was that expectant mothers were issued with the same distinctive green ration books that were allocated to children. (This made life hard for any woman who, for one reason or another, wished to keep her condition secret.) The green ration books contained special tokens, which allowed the mother-to-be extra milk at a reduced price, as well as extra coupons to help with the baby's needs.

During all or part of the period of 1950–54, meat, bacon, sugar, butter, tea, eggs, cheese and sweets were still rationed. In 1950 canned and dried fruit, chocolate biscuits, treacle, golden syrup, jellies and mincemeat had become available without points but supplies were still subject to availability; some parts of the country fared better than others – the equivalent of what in the twenty-first century has become known as the post-code lottery. Petrol and soap were also decontrolled later that year, so the mother-to-be was assured that she would have adequate supplies of soap flakes and washing powder to wash the nappies (or napkins) she would need in a few months' time.

Those nappies, as they were commonly called, made of terry towelling and fine muslin, were among the many other items that would be required. Few of those who were about to give birth at the very beginning of the 1950s had the luxury of going off with their husband to a specialist baby shop and buying whatever they fancied, or could afford, for the dreaded 'dockets' were still in existence. While most people are aware of the food rationing that existed during the Second World War, it may surprise some to learn that furniture was among many other commodities that could not be bought freely. During the war most manufacturers were directed to produce those items necessary to the war effort, while others were left struggling to produce essential goods against acute shortages of, in the case of furniture makers, both home-grown and imported timber. Thus there was very little new furniture available to meet the demands of those who had to replace the homes they had lost in the bombing, as well as those who were setting up home for the first time. So furniture rationing had been introduced under the government's Utility scheme. Selected manufacturers produced the best quality they could, using designs that harked back to the simplicity of the Arts and Crafts

A 1950s mother with her baby.

movement. All these pieces were marked with the CC41 Utility emblem.

The maximum number of units or dockets allowed to a married couple furnishing a new home was sixty, with another ten for each child. But since demand was so high not all the units were available for use straight away. Recipients would be informed when they might use them. For those young married couples who moved into two rooms in someone else's house, where they were expected to provide their own bedroom furniture, they would receive a maximum of twenty-five units which was sufficient for a large double bed, a wardrobe and a tall boy. Those moving into prefabricated houses with built-in furniture would have their allowance scaled down accordingly. The Board of Trade leaflet UFD/6 *Utility Furniture & Household Furnishings* makes awesome reading but does also throw light on the advantages and fairness of the scheme. To start with, all Utility furniture was free of purchase tax ($33\frac{1}{3}$ per cent at that time). There was a fixed maximum price for both new and second-hand pieces (which were also subject to units having to be surrendered), and traders were permitted to offer Utility furniture on hire purchase or credit sale agreements, provided that the full payment was made within two years.

Mattresses, bedding, curtains and flooring were all included in the scheme requiring units, but Utility nursery furniture, that is cots, playpens and high chairs, could be bought without a permit. However, the Board of Trade leaflet warned that as these were still in short supply there was little likelihood of there being enough for everyone who might need them. Therefore people were encouraged not to buy new chairs or cots, if they could make do with an old one, so prospective grandparents searched their lofts for any baby equipment that might be scrubbed, repainted, mended and brought back into service. Alternatively, the small advertisements in local newspapers and cards in shop windows proved a useful source for slightly more modern second-hand equipment for sale.

Clothes, too, continued to be rationed for a number of years after the war ended. The annual clothing coupon allowance had more than halved by 1945, which meant that the era of make-do-and-mend carried on well into the early 1950s. Girls who had learnt to knit socks and scarves for servicemen while they were at school were now making themselves jumpers and cardigans to wear for work. One clothing coupon was required for every 2oz of wool purchased. The only wool that did not require coupons was that designated as being for darning purposes. This came in small hanks made up of pieces cut to about 12–15in length. The ability to make a neat darn was a necessity in those days; if a sock wore thin at the heel, one either re-knitted the whole heel or carefully darned the thin area before the hole appeared, thus prolonging the life of the sock. Similarly, any other knitted garment that had a hole or a weak spot was repaired with a darn. The hanks of darning wool were sold in assorted colours, grey, brown, navy and black being the most popular, but white and pastel shades were also available for mending children's clothes. Such was the ingenuity of the women of the period that at Christmas many a little girl found her old doll had a new wardrobe of clothes: vest, knickers, jumper and skirt, coat, hat, socks and shoes, all knitted with strands of darning wool, carefully joined together. The basic navy of the main garments was enlivened by the introduction of inserts of a coloured pattern.

In the twenty-first century it is hard to believe that knitting wool was sold in 1oz skeins that had to be wound into balls before knitting could begin. 'Holding the wool' was an operation that was learnt by quite young schoolchildren. Though it was thought by many to be a tedious process as it meant sitting still for some time, for others it was an opportunity for a quiet chat. For those who have never seen the process, it went something like this. The skein holder and the winder sat facing each other about 2–3ft apart. The holder stretched out his or her arms with

A couple of skirts with two or three oversize blouses or smocks were usually sufficient to get the woman through the last few months.

the palms of the hands facing inwards, thumb erect. The winder, who was usually the knitter, then took the skein of wool, which was twisted in a loop, shook it out until it formed a circle and then placed that on to the holder's hands. It was essential that the holder kept the skein taut at all times. The winder, having located the beginning of the skein, started making her ball, carefully wrapping the wool a number of times over the fingers of one hand. When she was satisfied she had enough to form the centre of her ball, she slipped this off and continued winding until the skein was fully wound. It was necessary for the holder to develop a rhythm that matched that of the winder. This meant tilting the hands one way and then the other as the wool was wound. Woe betide – an expression much used in the 1950s – the holder who let the skein slacken or who failed to tilt at the right time. A knitter with no one available to help her wind was forced to make do with using the uprights of two kitchen or dining room chairs. With their backs facing and placed the correct distance apart to stretch the skein of wool, winding could commence, but it was an even more time-consuming process. How much better, if the young expectant mother could persuade the father-to-be to act as her holder – having first made sure that his hands were thoroughly clean!

As the mother-to-be progressed through her waiting time, the likelihood was that she would put on weight, though the powers-that-be urged her to disregard the old wives' tale that she should eat for two, stressing that her weight gain should be only a little more than the expected child would be. However, even if she did not put on a great deal of extra weight, her shape would alter significantly and eventually she would be forced to find new clothes suitable for her condition. In the January 1951 edition of *Mother* magazine, there appeared a knitting pattern for what was described as the 'cleverest maternity jumper'. Made with fine two-ply wool it had a lacy pattern. What earned it its superlative was the fact that it was knitted on a yoke onto which the two overlapping front pieces were pleated, thus allowing for, as the pattern had it, 'an adjustable bust measurement'.

In the 1950s there were no chain stores dedicated solely to the needs of mother and baby. Large department stores in towns and cities often had a nursery department but clothing for the expectant mother would, in the main, have formed part of the stock-in-trade of drapery and dress shops. As for baby clothes, these were often to be found in what were termed fancy goods shops, those that sold mainly wool or all things associated with embroidery. It was an appealing display in such a shop window that tempted Jean's husband to venture inside and buy the delicate little christening gown for his new daughter, an impulse buy that has had regular use within the family for sixty years.

In the main, most pregnant women did not spend a great deal on special maternity clothes. Wrap-around skirts were ideal for coping with an expanding waistline. The simplicity of their design meant they could be made at home or purchased at a reasonable price. A couple of skirts with two or three oversize blouses or smocks were usually sufficient to get the woman through the last few months. Some women resorted to wearing their husbands' shirts when they could no longer fit into their own clothes. Certain items of new underwear became essential as time progressed and there came a need for support garments too. But in many cases, the woman could get away with wearing her existing winter coat right to the end, especially if, like Mrs SJ's, it was one of those fashionable swagger coats which she had bought a couple of years earlier as part of her 'going away' outfit.

Most of the 1950s women continued at work for as long as possible for, as they were reminded by all the books and magazines of the period, as well as the staff at the antenatal clinic, 'Motherhood is a natural normal event and not an illness. Old wives' tales should be scorned as belonging to an ignorant past.' So wrote the sensible, down-to-earth Mabel Liddiard in *The Mothercraft Manual*. A State Registered Nurse and Midwife, Liddiard spent her life in maternity nursing, becoming nursing director of the Mothercraft Training Society, which was based on the principles of the late Truby King. The first of these was the importance of fresh air. The period up to and including the 1950s was obsessed with fresh air. The theory was that everyone, not just pregnant women, should spend as long as possible outside breathing in good, fresh air. One book actually stated that pregnant women needed to breathe for two, not eat for two! No matter what the weather, being outdoors was essential at some time during the day and linked with this was the necessity to take exercise. Being pregnant was not an excuse to stop taking part in sports if one normally played them, but every woman should take at least one walk a day regardless of weather; with stout shoes and warm clothing she would come to no harm. In fact she would be 'less likely to have colds than those who coddle themselves'. The emphasis on the importance of breathing fresh air was carried into the home and, in particular, to sleeping with the window open. Those of us who grew up in the 1940s and 1950s remember what it was like to sleep in a bedroom that was totally unheated in any case, yet was made even colder by your mother's insistence on having the window open at least 2in to allow the passage of fresh air in and the stale air out. This had, no doubt, been very sensible advice in the days when a bedroom accommodated five or six children in a small room.

The working woman who took plenty of exercise walking to and from work or when shopping daily – in all weathers – did her deep breathing and slept with the window open, should remain healthy and happy. Any minor complications or troubles that occurred were not natural but, said Liddiard, it was best to know a little about them and the example she cited was morning sickness. We of the late twentieth and early twenty-first centuries have been accustomed to film and TV depictions of a young woman hanging her head over a lavatory bowl as a way of conveying that she was pregnant. Liddiard would not have approved of this over-dramatisation. Listen to her no-nonsense sensible advice:

'Sometimes during the first three months there may be a feeling of nausea every morning and sometimes actual vomiting; this is commonly called "morning sickness". When this unpleasant condition exists it is best to have something to eat before rising and to get up slowly. *As little attention should be paid to it as possible;* it usually passes off after the first three months, if not sooner. Food should be taken as usual.'

She then goes on to recommend a successful cure: half a pint of milk mixed with half an ounce of Mead's *Casec or *Plasmon, to be taken before rising and last thing at night for three or four days. The two asterisks denoted that neither product could be obtained during wartime. The first, which seems to have been a form of magnesia, was imported from Canada, while the second came from Italy and is still used in prepared Italian baby foods.

Those who raised a wry smile at the foregoing, even thinking that Liddiard had obviously never experienced the condition herself, may be amused by a further direction that the mother-to-be should 'not give way to morbid cravings for one particular food about which there are many foolish superstitions'. We have all heard the apocryphal stories of the women who ate small pieces of coal or licked the distemper off the cowshed walls because they had a calcium deficiency or a need for charcoal in their diet, but there is no denying that most pregnant women do have sudden strange cravings for kippers or porridge, ice cream or salt and vinegar crisps. Liddiard uses the term 'morbid' in the medical sense of 'unwholesome'. Yet her advice on diet, generally, is wholly in accord with that of the present day: three well-balanced meals daily made up of a little meat, fish, eggs, cheese and butter, with plenty of vegetables, fresh fruit and salads. Tea and coffee were to be taken sparingly – many women in fact found that they became intolerant to both during pregnancy. Instead it was recommended that 1½–2 pints of milk should be taken each day in some form or another. On the subject of alcohol, Liddiard found it necessary to quote Sir Truby King himself:

> Alcohol taken by the mother flows as a poison in her blood. The tender growing cells of the baby, directly nourished by this poisoned stream, or fed with milk derived from it, do not grow or develop properly; they become stunted and degenerate. Therefore, an expectant or nursing mother should take no beer or stout, however strongly such drinks may be recommended by well-meaning friends or nurses.
>
> *Feeding and Care of Baby*

In fact during the 1950s nursing mothers were frequently offered glasses of stout during their stay in hospital.

The Mothercraft Manual first appeared in 1923, with the tenth edition being reprinted in 1946. (It was translated into Siamese in 1933, Chinese in 1935 and Afrikaans in 1937.) Thus this would have been the book most probably read by the parents of those who became mothers in the early 1950s and so would influence the well-meaning advice that they handed on. While much of the antenatal advice was sensible, if a trifle extreme, it has become a source of on-going debate over the years as to the value of the strictures laid down concerning the actual rearing of the infant. In the first half of the decade, the *Sunday Express* produced its own baby book. Mrs A.A. Woodman, MBE, SRN, SCM, certified health visitor, produced a handbook for mothers in response to what mothers had said they wanted to know. It was not just a reference book full of advice, but also included what, at that time, was a novel feature, namely a personal record section in which to chart the own child's progress.

It is interesting to compare the style and attitudes of Liddiard and Woodman. The former reflects the commonsense unemotional approach of the earlier period and was aimed at nursery nurses as well as mothers, while the latter is more sentimental. In the opening chapter of the *Sunday Express Baby Book* we are given the supposed thoughts of a mother-to-be including her dreams for the future of the child, based on the parental duty to teach and train it to grow up with high moral standards, which would be achieved with God's help. Today we might be surprised at the overt religious content but more shocking was the sexist attitude shown by the mother to her unborn child. She wishes that her daughter should be beautiful, since beauty is always an asset, provided it is more than skin deep. She wants her to be unselfish, loving, generous and kind – all things her parents can teach her. She must learn to be a sport and play the game by the rules. If she loses, then she must smile and try again. But it is the next wish that today's women may find irritating. There is nothing about the girl making the most of

And once she has found her man she must love him wholeheartedly; no matter what happens she must stick by him and trust him.

her ability and finding a satisfying career in which she could make use of all the goodness her parents have taught her; instead there is advice on what to look for in her search for a husband. The assumption is that this is every woman's ultimate aim. And once she has found her man she must love him wholeheartedly; no matter what happens she must stick by him and trust him. If things sometimes go wrong, she should just smile and love him all the more and things will come right again! As for her son, she wishes him to be honest, straightforward, kind and gentle. He must be fair in his dealings just as he would expect others to be. Again he, like the girl, must learn to be a good sport. The mother-to-be hopes he will never know poverty but, if he does, then he must have the courage to do the best he can with what he has. She hopes he will never be grumpy or cynical but always wear a cheerful grin on his face. When he comes to choose his partner in life, he must not be blinded by superficial appearances ... and so it goes on, and it is we the readers who become cynical, wondering in what ideal world this woman lives, knowing that she is more than likely to be in for a nasty shock one day.

However, once Mrs Woodman has left her hypothetical expectant mother, she too adopts a commonsense approach in the advice she gives, sometimes even echoing Liddiard. In the matter of sport, she advised that should be continued in moderation, although she believed swimming should be avoided on hygienic grounds. Unfortunately she does not specify what these were! Interestingly, she considered driving under the heading of sport and that too could be undertaken moderately. However, one should ask one's doctor when the baby was 6 months old if it was then permissible to start driving again. We may smile, but we have to remember that in the 1950s only a very small part of the female population could drive and of those, many did not have regular access to a car anyway because their husbands used it for work. Cars were still in short supply and new ones were very costly. It would be the 1960s and beyond before most families could afford one car let alone a second. Mrs Woodman also advised her readers to take two walks a day and to continue doing normal housework but avoiding heavy lifting and upward stretching. Like Liddiard she was obsessive about fresh air, sleeping with open windows and controlling one's weight.

Where the two diverged was on social life. Woodman thought one should continue with this as much as possible, as it gave the mother-to-be something else to think about, though of course the word moderation came into play here too. Late nights were to be avoided. More surprising were her views on smoking and drinking:

> Opinion is divided as to the effects of smoking during pregnancy. A cigarette now and then would seem to do no harm. If you are a heavy smoker, doctors advise that you cut down to a great extent, but you need not stop entirely, unless your doctor recommends it.

The progress of scientific research in recent years into the damage caused to health both by smoking and through the inhalation of stale cigarette smoke, has led to legislation on where it is now illegal to smoke. Had you told people in the 1950s that they would not be allowed to smoke while they watched a film at the cinema, and indeed at most places of entertainment, such as dance halls, they would have been aghast. Smoking was not just fashionable, as most of the cigarette advertisements of the time showed, it also cut right across the social classes; the working man lit up his cigarette in the pub while those dining out in a restaurant thought nothing of smoking between courses if they could not wait until their coffee was served. Once the Loyal Toast had been drunk at formal dinners, the Master of Ceremonies would announce: 'you may now smoke.' Films of the period, whether they were romances or thrillers, used cigarettes to define characters or to create atmosphere, and thus indirectly encouraged smoking. The overflowing ashtray was to be found in offices of all sorts from solicitors to head-teachers: on the counters of some shops and even on the desk of the doctor himself. Many a young mother-to-be attending her first check-up might well have been cautioned to cut down on her smoking by a GP who reeked of stale smoke and whose fingers bore telltale nicotine stains. Few, we hope, had a similar experience to that of Diana. Married in 1953, after a whirlwind courtship, she set up home in Nigeria where her husband worked. When she became pregnant she came under the care of an English doctor who worked at the local hospital. He was a charming man but Diana did find his chain smoking while he delivered her baby off putting to say the least. As she commented when relating this story, nowadays one would have asked him to stop, but in those days, well she was young, and in any case it was all part of accepted behaviour.

As for alcohol, 1950s women certainly did not drink as much as they do now. Wine imports from Europe were still in short supply and expensive, so wine drinking tended to be limited to special occasions like weddings and to accompany Christmas lunch. Cheaper brands of sherry and port would appear around Christmas, but on the whole when women drank outside the home they tended to have such things as a lemonade shandy, the exciting new fizzy Babycham, or diluted spirits in the form of port with lemonade, or gin with neat orange squash or lime juice. Mrs Woodman perhaps reveals unwittingly the intended market for the *Sunday Express*

Baby Book when she wrote, 'Alcoholic drinks place an added strain on the kidneys at this time and should be indulged in rarely, if at all. Your doctor may permit an occasional cocktail but any more than this may do definite damage.' So the occasional martini or Manhattan could be served for these ladies.

Had she been writing today, Mrs Woodman no doubt would have commented on the increase in obesity generally in many parts of the western world. In 1950 she warned, as Liddiard had done, that pregnancy was not an excuse to overeat:

> True, you are eating for your baby as well as yourself, yet you must not get too fat. Fat increases the difficulties of delivery and is mighty hard to get rid of afterwards! The up-to-date doctor therefore sees that the expectant mothers are weighed when they come for their regular examinations, and in most cases insists that they do not gain more than 25 pounds.

That was rather more than Truby King or Miss Liddiard would have allowed.

The early years of the National Health Service offered the 1950s expectant mother good antenatal care. For the first time, all this care was free; those who in the past had been unable to afford medical treatment now saw a doctor regularly, with visits in between to midwives at the local clinic. Any worries that the mother-to-be had could be dealt with promptly. Had she been one of those who had neglected to have dental treatment because of the cost, she now had no excuse not to visit the dentist because that too was provided free by the NHS. One of the first things to be decided once the expected date of birth was confirmed was where it should take place. In the past it had been accepted that most women had their babies at home but during the 1950s there was a definite move on the part of the NHS to encourage hospital confinements. There were many good reasons for this, starting with the fact that both doctors and midwives were always on hand, whereas they might be delayed when a home birth was imminent. There were other reasons that would not apply today. We must remember that the housing conditions of a large part of the population were often vastly overcrowded. There were still people living in rows of back-to-back houses where the lavatory block in the communal courtyard was shared by all the neighbours and the only water supply was a single cold tap in the small back kitchen. Unbelievable now, there were council houses dating from the late 1920s that had been built with an outside lavatory only. Tenants were still expected to take their weekly bath in a tin bath brought into the kitchen or living room. Those in the country often had neither running water nor mains drainage.

True, you are eating for your baby as well as yourself, yet you must not get too fat.

In an age which had advanced medically, hygiene was of paramount importance. Many of the women who contributed information for this book and its predecessor, *A 1950s Housewife*, were living in two rooms, which they rented in someone else's home, where facilities for giving birth were not ideal. This was not the same as living in a family home where mum or the next-door neighbours might be called upon to help. The landlady might be prepared to put up with her tenant's new baby when it did arrive but she certainly did not want all and sundry tramping through her home for the birth. Most of the contributors in this situation were living in reasonable surroundings where they were the only tenants, but there were a great many women, mainly in the larger towns and cities, who were living in large old houses where several families were housed, again having to share one lavatory between them and where access to a bathroom was given only on additional payment. Much better, therefore, to admit the expectant mother to the maternity ward or nursing home where she could be carefully monitored both before and after the birth.

Before the introduction of the National Health Service, hospitals had catered for those who were in need of surgery or were seriously ill. They also ran an out-patients' department where patients came for consultations with specialists. Most also had a small ward for sick children but few, except in very large towns and cities, had a designated maternity unit for straightforward confinements. Only those women who developed complications were admitted to hospital, so when it became accepted they should have their babies in a hospital environment rather than at home, it was necessary to find extra accommodation. Since building work was still severely restricted at the time, existing buildings were adapted and in some cases the small private nursing homes that already existed were taken over and enlarged, and those patients whose home conditions were considered unsuitable for a home birth were booked in there. For those women who felt happier having their baby in a nursing home but who did not meet the lack of home facilities criteria, the private nursing home was still available – at a price, as the illustration on p37–8 shows.

Where, you may ask, did the expectant father fit into all this? In a hospital situation he was most definitely excluded from the actual birth. Liddiard mentions husbands along with friends, who 'should do all in their power to make her [the expectant mother's] life happy, free from worry, and full of loving companionship'. But that was during the waiting period. Woodman deals with the subject of what father should do once he has delivered his wife to the hospital. He will, she says, be advised that it will be some time before anything happens, so he should go home or back to the office. If he insists on staying then he may do so in the waiting room. Eventually he will be informed of the baby's arrival but, she warns the new mother, 'You may slip into sleep so quickly that you will not even be aware of proud father – if he is allowed to come into your room for a moment to see you'. What Liddiard and Woodman would have thought of men being present at the birth, holding their wife's hand and encouraging her with her breathing, I think we can guess. Certainly in the 1950s having a baby was very much 'women's business' and this exclusion from the birth may account for why it took many men of that generation time to bond with their children.

2

The New Baby Needs ...

*B*abies cost a fortune! A headline like that or something similar appears with monotonous regularity every few years, as the cost of providing the basic equipment and clothing for a baby rises. In the same way that the modern wedding, as opposed to one in the 1950s, costs a fortune because of the wide choice of options available, so too is the modern mother confronted with a huge and tempting array of articles for baby that would have amazed her grandmother. Babies of the 1950s were, in the main, dressed in what could be termed as the baby's uniform. Every mother-to-be was advised to prepare a layette; a term that encompassed the clothing, bedding and toiletry needs of the newborn. As far as Mrs Woodman was concerned, baby's clothing could not have been simpler; summer or winter it was the basic vest and nappie. Her statement that 'The old custom of swathing the tiny baby in wool and flannel even in hot weather has fortunately gone out', was indeed partially true at the time but what would she have thought of the article in *The Daily Telegraph*, 20 December 2011, headlined: 'Swaddling newborn babies comes back into fashion after fifty years'. Apparently Debenhams stores reported a 61 per cent increase in the sale of swaddling clothes in that year. The modern view in the 1950s was that baby needed to be kept warm and fit, not heavily weighed down with clothing. However, it had to be recognised that much would depend upon where one lived and the heating arrangements within the home. the *Sunday Express Baby Book* essentials for baby's wardrobe were:

4 sleeveless or long-sleeved vests – cotton, silk or wool – depending on season and warmth of the home

4 short or long nightgowns (fine woollen material for winter, cotton crepe for summer)

4 day gowns of woollen or cotton material

4 matinee coats (woollen)

leggings

overalls

bonnet

bootees

gloves

2 carrying shawls

1 cloak

1 hood

4 dozen napkins

Contrast this with Liddiard's list of essentials:

> 4 vests (silk or wool)
> 4 cellular shirts if using woollen vests
> 4 petticoats
> 4 frocks [for babies of either sex]
> 3 coats (flannel or knitted)
> 4 nightgowns
> 4 pairs of bootees
> 1 large shawl
> 2 small soft shawls
> 6 bibs
> 2 dozen Harringtons napkins (those made of muslin)
> 2 dozen Turkish towelling napkins
> 1/2 dozen small handkerchiefs (kept for baby's own use)

Much of the actual knitted goods would have been either home-made or received as gifts, but there was still the expense of buying those four dozen nappies. What a good thing that the government was now providing a maternity grant for the new mother. The sum of £4 would not purchase much today but it certainly helped at a time when a basic weekly wage was only a pound or two more than that. Added to which, the mother who had managed to stay at work until six weeks before the birth of her child was entitled to a weekly allowance of £3 6s 0d for those six weeks and the following thirteen. These amounts would have been helpful perhaps as down payments on a pram or towards the purchase of essential items. Certainly the government had not intended that maternity allowances should be used as the down payment on the television set that was installed in time for the Coronation in 1953, as was confided by one '1950s child', with the excuse that as the family already had several children there were plenty of hand-me-downs that could be used for the new addition.

An additional item advocated by Miss Liddiard for those occasions when baby was being carried was 'a pair of little drawers or a pilch [usually knitted] to be worn' over the nappie. But, she warns, 'the mack-intosh drawers so much advertised cannot be too severely condemned. They are non-porous, allow of no ventilation; their use means enclosing the wet nappy with all its impurities against the skin ... From every point of view their use is bad.' Having digested that, what naïve young mother would dare to use them even though it meant changing her baby more often? Mrs Woodman, however, believed it was quite in order to leave the baby wet between feeds. We presume that these 'mackintosh drawers' were rubberised and were the precursor of the plastic pants of the 1950s. These, while very useful, did, after time and much washing, become rather brittle. Diana related that while she was living in Nigeria she ordered a pair of rubberised water-proof pants to be sent out from London for her little girl. Diana had the luxury of a local nanny who, having been trained in all aspects of baby-care including the baby's laundry, unfortunately meticulously ironed this precious pair of pants! Something that may come as a surprise to many of those who were 1950s mothers is the disposable nappy. There were apparently several brands available then although not widely known. Woodman recommended that, whether or not they were used regularly, it was good to have a supply on hand for those times when the mother was either ill or too busy, when it was sensible for her to conserve her strength by omitting the trouble of washing nappies. Only one of my contributors mentioned using the disposable Paddi-pads. These were, as their name implies, pads that fitted into plastic pants. Mollie's decision to use them was forced upon her because she was living in rented rooms where there were no facilities in the shared kitchen to boil soiled nappies.

The books of advice also gave detailed instructions on the baby's sleeping arrangements. All agreed that the first cradle or crib did not need to be elaborate; it could be a basket cot with or without a stand. In fact, many newborn babies started life in a wickerwork laundry basket, carefully lined to make sure that the infant was never in danger of being scratched. If the baby arrived unexpectedly before a cradle had been prepared, the bottom drawer of a chest of drawers was

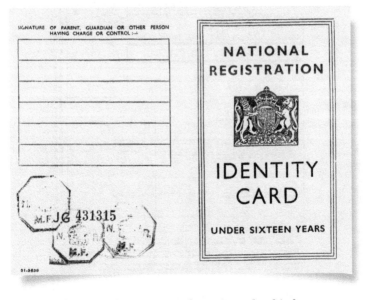

A national identity card was issued at birth.

often pressed into service. That, like the basket, was to be placed safely on two chairs, never on the floor because of draughts. Many young parents opted for the convenience of a carrycot which, as its name suggested, could be taken out and about, either carried by its two handles or placed into a wheeled frame which turned it into a pram.

All the books of the period stated categorically that the baby should have a room of its own right from the start, in order to help the infant build good sleeping habits and to give the mother more rest. The size of

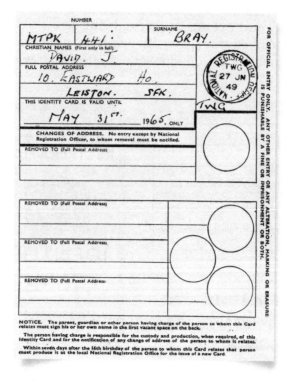

The details contained on the national identity card.

the baby's room was unimportant as long as it was well ventilated and quiet. During the first few weeks, however, it was better if the baby was in a room adjoining the mother's (or some other responsible person) who would be able to hear if the baby cried and could give it attention. The latter advice must surely have been aimed at those who could afford to have a live-in maternity nurse for six weeks to three months. That, of course, was not an option for most new mothers, and for those in limited accommodation neither was a separate room. However, the experts had an answer for that too! During the day, the parental bedroom could become baby's nursery and, at night, his cradle was carried or wheeled into the living room. As one 1950s mother remarked on hearing this advice: what happened if your two rented rooms were on different floors? It was essential that in whichever room the baby was, the temperature should not go below 60°F (15°C) during the night and 65°F(18°F) during the day. On paper this sounds fine but with hindsight how many babies were wheeled from their parents' bedroom after the late evening feed, into a room that had been occupied all day in which smoking may have taken place and was not properly ventilated? One has a mental picture of windows being flung open to give the ventilation required but perhaps reduce the temperature in the room.

For the first-time mother all the advice she received from kindly relatives and friends, midwives and health visitors, as well as that which she read in books and magazines, must have been daunting. There must have been times when she thought to herself, it cannot be that difficult, people have been bringing up babies since human life began. Was it really necessary that she had to have all the bits and pieces the books suggested? Did she really have to furnish a nursery in a room that faced south, with a cot, a screen and a bath; a chest of drawers or a wardrobe that had drawers; a small medicine cupboard in which to keep all the bath-time requisites; a low chair without arms for nursing and bathing; a small towel horse and a firm wooden table? The sensible answer for most people was no, of course you didn't! Every mother eventually found her own way of doing things. Probably the most disregarded piece of advice was to put the baby into a room of its own straight away. Start as you mean to go on to establish good habits may be sound advice on paper or from those who did not have to get up in the middle of a cold winter's night in an unheated house and pad along half asleep to attend to a crying infant and then sit and feed the child. 'The carrycot was in our room as it was more convenient and as we lived in a house with no heating it saved walking about in the cold.' Vera's experience was echoed by most of the contributors; in fact not one mentioned the baby being in a separate room. But, our experts would cry, start as you mean to go on and there was no need for baby to be fed through the night.

A baby brought up on the teachings of Dr Truby King did not eat between midnight and sunrise. According to him night feeds were unnatural as well as taxing for the mother. The baby should sleep for eight hours at a stretch in natural darkness. During the day the child should receive four-hourly feeds but after the last evening one, should the baby wake during the night and cry, it should be changed if it was wet, and then tucked up warmly in the cot. If the crying persisted then warm boiled water *without* sugar should be given. Then followed the most important stricture: 'The baby must *never* be taken into the mother's or nurse's bed.'

All very well but few mothers had a maternity nurse who 'should be willing to have a few disturbed nights in order that the baby may be trained to sleep for eight hours at a stretch'.

The young first-time mother probably spent eight to ten days in hospital or a nursing home following the birth. Although all the advice of the time was that childbirth was natural and not in any way to be treated like an illness, the woman was certainly not encouraged to exert herself too much, often remaining confined to bed for two or three days before being allowed up. One wonders what the likes of Liddiard and Woodman would have made of the mother who has her baby in hospital these days and then is allowed home within hours of the birth. Back in the 1950s the NHS gave some new mothers what amounted to a short holiday. Although good in some respects, in others it put off the day when the mother would have to cope with her new responsibility. To start with, in some hospitals or nursing homes, all the new babies were kept in the nursery, being brought out only at regular intervals for the mothers to feed. This meant that the babies were already being trained to take food at four-hourly intervals. The drawback was that some infants were not properly awake when brought to mother and were likely to continue sleeping in her arms rather than eagerly sucking from the breast. Hard luck then when it was time for the babies to be returned to the nursery. That child would go back hungry. When he did decide it was time for him to eat, rather than disturb the routine of the ward, the nurses would give him a bottle in the nursery. Mothers were often not told that this was happening but it meant that regardless of the mothers' wishes, the babies would find it easier to take a bottle rather than struggle with the breast. Many women

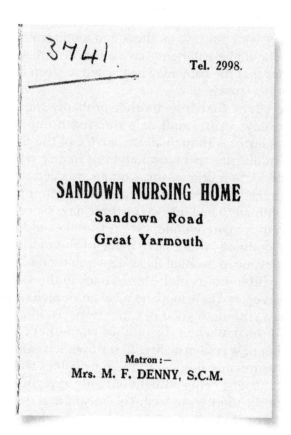

A brochure for a private nursing home.

found the first few days of breast-feeding very difficult and the staff in the nursing home were not always as sympathetic as they might have been in helping the new mother who wanted to persevere with feeding the baby herself.

Bonding with baby is a concept that was never articulated in the 1950s. We have mentioned in passing how alien the idea that the father should be present at the birth and thus witness the event in all

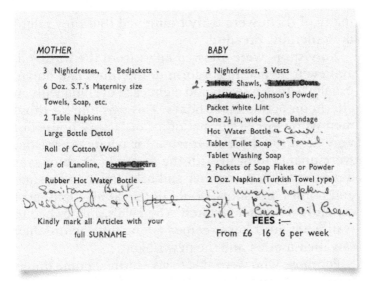

MOTHER	BABY
3 Nightdresses, 2 Bedjackets .	3 Nightdresses, 3 Vests
6 Doz. S.T.'s Maternity size	~~3 Head~~ Shawls, ~~3 Wool Coats~~
Towels, Soap, etc.	~~Jar of Vaseline~~, Johnson's Powder
	Packet white Lint
2 Table Napkins	One 2½ in, wide Crepe Bandage
Large Bottle Dettol	Hot Water Bottle *& Cover* .
Roll of Cotton Wool	Tablet Toilet Soap *& Towel* .
	Tablet Washing Soap
Jar of Lanoline, ~~Bottle Cascara~~	2 Packets of Soap Flakes or Powder
Rubber Hot Water Bottle .	2 Doz. Napkins (Turkish Towel type)
Sanitary Belt	*muslin napkins*
Dressing Gown & Slippers.	*Soapy Pins*
	Zinc & Castor oil Cream
Kindly mark all Articles with your	**FEES :—**
full SURNAME	From £6 16 6 per week

What mother had to take with her.

its gory glory. The Liddiards and Woodmans and their
ilk would have been horrified at the very idea, let
alone a father being able to hold his newborn child
within minutes of its arrival. For the women who had
their babies in those years, they too were restricted as
to how much contact they had with the baby during
the first week or so. While the intention was to make
sure that the mother was given the chance to rest
thoroughly and recoup her strength, many felt frustrated that they could not see their baby when they
wished. Mothers only got to hold their babies when
they fed them or towards the end of the confinement period when they changed nappies and were
shown how to bath the baby. With so little chance to
handle their baby it is small wonder that when they
suddenly found themselves alone with him at home,

many of them were truly frightened that they might do something dreadful.

No visitors were allowed apart from the husband, and even he had to conform to the times laid down, usually between seven and eight each evening with an afternoon period on Sundays. This was fine for those men who worked normal office or factory hours but very hard for those men who, for whatever reason, were unable to fit in with the norm. Everything was done to keep both mother and baby quiet and rested, and hordes of visitors would not do at all – and most certainly not other children! The 1950s siblings had to wait what must have seemed a long time before they saw their mother and the new sibling.

For those who were able to give birth at home things were much more relaxed. During their visits to the antenatal clinic they should have built up a rapport with their midwifery team, one of whom was likely to be on duty when she was needed. The midwife would have visited the home and assessed if she had every-thing she needed, at the same time learning more about the background of her patient. She would also discover and most probably meet the expectant mother's own mother or mother-in-law, who would be looking after her. Sometimes this might be a neighbour instead, better still if she was a woman who had had experi-ence of attending births and would not panic should anything be amiss. Once the baby was born, then the chances were that the baby remained very close to its mother, even if the modern thinking of that time decreed it should be kept quiet, in another room, away from visitors. There was little chance of any of that in a busy family or a house with multiple occupation.

Although being able to have one's baby at home seemed to be more natural, there were considerations

Baby's 'play time'. Note the lovely knitted shawl.

to be taken into account. One of these was the importance of having someone the mother-to-be could rely
on to make the important telephone call to alert the
midwife. In the 1950s very few homes were connected
to the telephone system, so when the time came who-
ever was deputed to make the call had to ensure that
they had enough small change with them when they
went to the nearest public telephone box. Once the
midwife had been told or a message passed to her, it
was a question of waiting for her to arrive. This could be
a worrying time for both father and mother, especially
if it was the middle of the night. Once the midwife had
visited and examined the woman, she would decide
how imminent the birth was. If it was thought to be
some time off, she might leave to visit another case.
Sometimes, by the time the midwife arrived, the baby

was almost here, or in some cases, had actually made its debut. Most home births were straightforward but occasionally complications did occur both before and after the delivery. Let Mrs W tell what happened to her:

> Baby was born at about 10.00 on 6 June 1950. He was born at the home of his grandparents where we had two rooms, as there was a housing shortage after the war. Midwife came early morning, then found he was breech so she had to call Doctor. But when he came he hadn't experienced a breech baby so he had to call another doctor. But the second came just as forceps were used. One of the doctors asked if I was Princess Elizabeth because she had several doctors [when her children were delivered]. Baby was delivered bottom first. Baby wouldn't feed so I had to extract milk from breast and feed him with a drip feeder. After three days a child specialist came down from the hospital [in the county town] to see the baby. He pushed his legs up and down, then said 'no baby died with starvation'. After the exercise baby started sucking normally.

Mrs W commented after this account that it was all a bit traumatic. A masterpiece of understatement as one considers what was going on. Again we have to remind ourselves that in those telephone-less, let alone mobile phone-owning days, someone would have had to go out to call the first doctor and then again for the second one, all of which must have taken a worrying length of time. So it was hardly surprising that by the time the second doctor arrived the baby needed to be delivered with the use of forceps. We also assume nowadays that our GPs are fully competent to deal with all emergencies, so the first doctor's inexperience comes as a shock.

We can imagine some of Mrs W's anxiety, in those three days after the birth, at her baby's inability to feed, even though she would have been supported by the daily visits from her midwife. It says much for the new National Health Service that a consultant paediatrician travelled from the hospital in one town to another town, 20 or so miles away, to examine the baby of an ordinary couple in their home.

3

Baby and Mother Should Live by the Clock

A baby differs from the suckling animal or from the baby of the uncivilised savage in that, as he grows up, his meal-time, sleep-time, play-time, and work-time will be determined by social circumstances. The careless, shiftless and ignorant mother, whose child is brought up without method, and given the breast whenever he cries for it, is injuring both the health and character of her child. Not only is he likely to have disturbed digestion and irregularities in the action of the bowels but he is acquiring the slipshod ways of his parents and without discipline in self-control, he grows up self-willed and unable to adapt himself to our customs, and is neither physically nor morally a credit to the race.

Dr Fairbairn, *'A Text Book for Midwives'*,
in *The Mothercraft Manual*

Pity the poor new mother who came across this quotation in *The Mothercraft Manual*. It was enough to fill her with dread at the enormity of the task before her in raising a child, as well as being a dire warning that if she did not obey the rules she would not only ruin her child physically and morally, but she would be labelled as a useless mother. There was no way she wished to be called careless, shiftless and ignorant, still worse to be equated with the uncivilised savage. That phrase alone tells us much about the imperialistic and prejudiced attitudes that still lingered in the 1950s, as does the reference to the irregularities of the bowels. It used to be a standing joke with our European neighbours that the English were obsessed with their bowels and their need to take medicaments that would 'keep them regular'. This emphasis on the bowels led to the rebellion against early 'potty training', which raged in the 1960s – but more of that later.

It is possible that while she was resting in bed on the third or fourth day after the birth of her child, when the initial euphoria had worn off, the young woman had time to think of what lay before her. She might have spent the last six years or so in a busy office pounding a manual typewriter and taking dictation in shorthand from one of the male managers or she had learnt to operate a comptometer, that miracle machine which allowed all sorts of mathematical calculations to be performed without the use of pen and paper. She had, perhaps, been a hairdresser, worked in a shop or trained as a nurse or a teacher, but no matter what form her employment took, she had received training that allowed her to perform the best she could. And now? Here she was – a mother! How on earth was she going to take on what amounted to a job for life? This was not a position with fixed hours – she could not put a cover over a baby at half past five in the afternoon as she did on her typewriter and then go home. Neither could she, if she decided that this job was not to her liking, give in her notice and find something else. True she had not had 'proper training' for motherhood but plenty of help was on hand with other women, mid-wives, health visitors, books and magazines, all eager to pass on useful tips on how it should be done. The problem was where to start and who to listen to.

A careful reading of *The Mothercraft Manual* was enough to convince the average new mother that this was like being back at school lectured by the severe schoolmarm with small round tortoiseshell glasses and hair scraped back in a bun, holding a thin cane that she tapped against the salient points on the blackboard. You half expected to feel the cane across your knuck-les if you failed to carry out the instructions in the manual. Much gentler and more reassuring was the sensible advice given in the *Sunday Express Baby Book*. In the chapter headed 'Your Baby from Birth to One Month', the mother found answers to such questions as how much should the baby eat, how to encourage it to suckle and what do you do if that proved diffi-cult. The editor mentions that because in the 1930s and 1940s good substitutes for breast milk had become available, many mothers had been persuaded to use them in a bottle rather than the natural supply. There were several reasons why this had happened some women found the initial period of waiting for lactation to take place so painful that they turned immediately to the bottle; others found that after a few weeks their milk supply was not sufficient to satisfy their hungry infant and so they were forced to use cows' or goats' milk or a dried milk formula. The most usual reason for opting for the bottle was convenience. Anyone could give the baby its feed in a bottle – even father – so if mother was leading a very busy life, either returning to work or following a demanding social life, then bottles were the answer.

The Mothercraft Manual described the use of powdered milk as 'artificial or unnatural feeding', so strongly did the author feel on the subject that the chapter she devoted to it was, she said, for the benefit of 'those unfortunate infants who lost their mothers at birth'. The chapter is long and involved citing scientific studies, including tables for using cows' milk modified with lime-water or boiled water. Sugar and cream, unsweetened condensed milk and dried milk were similarly treated. She then entered a warning about the necessity of having a dairy thermometer to test the heated milk since what would be the correct temperature for a baby to suck would seem almost cold to an adult. Having absorbed this knowledge the reader was then instructed how to sterilise bottles and teats, and as if to rub in the expense of this unnatural form of feeding, she advises one should have as many bottles as one gave feeds daily. Yet in spite of these warnings, there was a definite increase in bottle-feeding during the 1930s when some mothers boasted of having a 'Cow and Gate' baby. Was it just a fashion? Or was it that in the dark days of the Depression many women whose husbands were unemployed were forced to take work outside the home to keep their households running?

However, by the 1950s there was a distinct move in some quarters to encourage breast-feeding. Among the arguments put forward were that infant mortality was less amongst breast-fed babies who acquired immunity to disease from their mother's milk, while for the mother herself the process aided a more speedy return of her internal organs to normality. The breast-fed

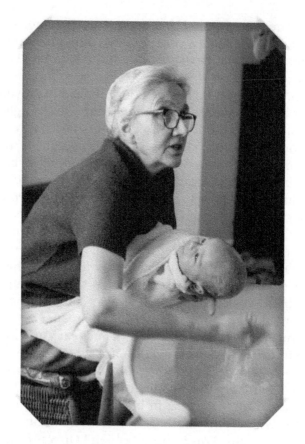

Granny shows how it should be done.

child had to work harder to get its milk than the baby
sucking on a rubber teat, and since, it was claimed,
every baby needed and craved a certain amount of
sucking time, the bottle-fed infant would compensate
by sucking his thumb, fingers or blankets. We shall
hear more on this subject later, but suffice to say that
most mothers have long since disproved this particular
theory. The other great advantage for natural feeding

was that it was cheap and always available. Unlike bottles it required no time-consuming sterilisation procedure, it was always at the correct temperature and in those days before everyone had a refrigerator, there was no fear that the milk would go off. Since all babies were entitled to supplies of National Dried Milk at a reduced price, could it be that there was an economic reason behind the push towards breast-feeding? It was surprising, however, to discover that in some quarters there was a deeply ingrained antipathy towards natural feeding in the previous generation; one contributor reported her deep hurt when her mother-in-law expressed the opinion that the practice 'Was barbaric and she was no better than an animal'.

Unfortunately, looking back it seems that there was reluctance on the part of society in general to accept that breast-feeding was a natural process and that when a baby cried it might be a sign that it was time to be fed. There was no provision in public places for a nursing mother; a woman who tucked herself away in the corner of a café and discreetly put her baby to the breast was likely to be ordered to leave. But this embargo on openly feeding reached into private homes too. Many older women thought it wrong that male members of the family and younger children should witness the process so they banished the young mother to another room, using the excuse that no doubt the mother would prefer her privacy. One can understand, perhaps, why changing a heavily soiled nappy in someone else's sitting room might not be socially acceptable, but why should revealing a small portion of a breast be so wrong? Outside the home, a 1950s mother who found herself forced to remove her baby's nappy and put on a clean one would have had to make use of a public lavatory. These varied greatly in cleanliness, so one just hoped the one chosen was not only clean but also had an attendant who might allow the mother to sit down on her chair while she changed the nappy. It was not an experience the mother would wish to repeat often since it made her feel embarrassed and inferior. This was odd, really, considering that most of the other women she encountered in the public conveniences were likely to have been or would become mothers themselves.

Neither of the aforementioned situations was discussed in the *Sunday Express Baby Book*. In contrast to Liddiard's book, this gave much simpler but nonetheless sensible and reassuring advice, such as why it was essential to hold the baby up against your shoulder to expel air after it had been fed; when to change nappies; how to give a bath; and what you should do when the baby cried. Perhaps the most comforting words came in the section 'A Timetable to Fit Your Baby'. Here Mrs Woodman stated that many mothers were confused by the timetables they were given and tried to make their baby conform to it believing that when the baby cried with hunger at 9.30, she must wait until the clock strikes 10 before feeding him, because that is what the book says. Learn to be flexible, she advises, and do not let baby wear himself out with crying. Interestingly the writer was anticipating the strong movement that emerged in the 1960s when she wrote: 'Difficulties caused by over-tenseness on the mother's part, or timetables that do not fit, have stirred up some

> *As far as nappy changing was concerned, there were no designated public facilities for this purpose.*

rebellion lately against any table at all.' (Sharp intake of breath on the part of earlier writers on the subject!) However, Mrs Woodman continues, 'This is not as horrifying as it sounds, for baby will quickly establish his own time, which will be the one best suited to his own intestinal rhythm.'

The timetable she prescribed started when the baby was 2 weeks old; she was presuming that a routine of sorts as far as feeding was concerned would already have been established by the hospital or the nurse at home. So her suggestion was as follows:

6 a.m. Breast (or bottle feeding) ten to twelve minutes at first, increasing as baby gets stronger. After feeding, make bed and baby dry and clean, then put him back to bed.

9 a.m. Bath.

10 a.m. Feed.

10.30 a.m. to 2 p.m. Nap in his own room, with door shut and window open. The temperature must not fall below 60°F(15°C).

2 p.m. Feed.

3 p.m. to 4 p.m. Airing, out of doors when the baby is past 2 to 3 weeks old and the weather is not stormy or too cold. Otherwise, in the bedroom.

5 p.m. to 6 p.m. Exercise period. Fun for all! Put baby on your big bed with all his clothing except his napkin removed. (Have a large thick pad over the bed to protect it.) The room temperature should be warm. Let baby kick freely. It is a fine idea to massage his back and hold him during the last half hour of this period. Visit with him, love him, carry him about the house. This will rest him for the night. Do not bounce him or throw him around, however. That comes under the head of

over-stimulation and interferes with the sleep and
digestion of most babies.

6 p.m. Feed. Put on his nightgown and return him
to bed in a room by himself with the door closed,
light out and window open. Temperature no lower
than 60°F (15°C).

10 p.m. Feed.

2 a.m. Feed if baby wakens and seems to need it.
Do not wake him for it. This feeding is eliminated
when he is 6–7 weeks old.

This is all very straight forward. The woman who
followed it to the letter might have needed reminding that she had to change nappies when necessary,
as there is only one reference to making the baby
clean and dry. When asked what help and advice they
received, most women replied that they used their
common sense which proved a great standby. In the
hours between feeds the mother found time to do
her housework, laundry and cooking. And once the
baby could be taken outside, that was when she got
her exercise and daily dose of fresh air by pushing
the pram to the shops to buy her groceries. One wonders what the baby-care experts of the 1950s would
have thought if they had witnessed a common sight
today of a young mother with a baby, not more than
a week old, tucked up in a curved baby seat, perched
in a supermarket trolley. The midwives would have
thrown up their hands in horror that the mother was
behaving as if she had not just given birth and the
baby specialists would have been equally aghast at the
infant being exposed to the over-stimulation of the
noise and bright lights so early in its life, not to mention the dangers of infection from the adult strangers
who stopped to admire it.

There has been growing concern in medical circles during the present decade at the increase of vitamin D deficiency in both children and adults, resulting in a renewal of conditions that were thought to belong to the past. The lack of vitamin D had been identified as being the major cause in Victorian times of rickets, a condition that resulted in the sufferer having softened bones. Those who grew up in the 1930s would have been accustomed to seeing children wearing leg braces which were designed to correct the soft bones that had grown twisted. During the 1940s the disease was thought to have been eradicated, mainly due to the addition of many vitamins to foodstuffs. In primary schools, children thought to be at risk were given a daily dose of cod liver oil and malt, while all expectant mothers were issued with vitamin supplements that included C, in their concentrated orange juice, and A and D found in fish oil capsules, which were taken for their own benefit as well as their forthcoming child's. Once the baby was born, whether he was being fed on breast or bottle milk, he needed to have these added supplements. Discussing vitamin D, Mrs Woodman made the point that the livers of other fish as well as cod were being used in the oil for babies and that it was best to use a pure, unflavoured variety. As many mothers were put off by the smell of cod liver oil, it was to be hoped that pure fish oil was also free from smell. But how on earth was the new mother to get the recommended dose of five to ten drops, twice a day, into her little one? Gently but firmly – as indeed

> *As many mothers were put off by the smell of cod liver oil, it was to be hoped that pure fish oil was also free from smell.*

was Mrs Woodman's advice – one needed to have the
baby lying either on the bath table or against your arm
and then 'You may gently press his mouth open with
thumb and finger against his cheeks, then slip the oil
over his tongue and into the back of his mouth. Be very
gentle but insist that it goes down. Babies usually love
the oil after they get used to it, but whether he likes it
or not, he has to have it, for teeth, bones and general
well-being.' In other words, he was learning very early
to appreciate that some things that seemed unpalatable
really were 'good for you'!

The natural source of vitamin D is sunlight, and here
all the experts from Truby King onward were in agreement. Babies and young children should spend as
much time as possible outside in the fresh air because
it was believed that daily exposure to fresh air and
sunshine increased appetite and encouraged growth.
Miss Liddiard placed her babies either outside, which
she called her day nursery, or indoors beside an open
window depending on the weather throughout the
day, while Mrs Woodman's regime opted for mid afternoon. After their babies were bathed and fed in the
morning, most mothers in the 1950s (and 1960s too)
placed their babies outside in the pram, if it was neither too wet nor too cold, and again in the afternoon
if they did not go out for a walk. Once the weather
warmed up around the beginning of May, mothers
were encouraged to let the baby sunbathe. Starting
with two minutes each on his front and back wearing only his nappy, and slowly increasing the time
exposed to the sun's rays, by late May the baby would
have acquired a tan. However, there was a warning
of the danger of exposing the child to the midsum-
mer sun. When in the pram a canopy should be used
to protect the infant's eyes as well as his body, and if

he were lying on a rug in the garden then a parasol should provide protection.

One of the interesting features in the *Sunday Express Baby Book* that shows a softening in the rigidity of previous ideas on bringing up a baby, was the hour between five and six which the author called exercise time but subtitled, 'fun for all'. This was the time when perhaps, though he is not actually mentioned, father might be home from work and have the opportunity to play with the baby. Modern readers might be puzzled with the injunction to 'visit with him, love him'. In the past there were experts who believed that all you need do was keep an infant clean, comfortable and well fed. During feeding the child was held close to the mother but the idea of playing with it and cuddling it in between feeds was

'If you pick him up and cuddle him, he'll expect it all the time.'

disapproved of. Mrs Woodman writes a telling statement when discussing crying: 'For some years experts advised mothers not to pick up baby when it cried. Now [1950] they have relented. Baby should be comforted but not spoilt.' Even the gentle Mrs Woodman had been imbued with the old ideas of spare the rod. Yet a mother instinctively responds to her baby's cry and it is natural that she should pick up the child in order to determine the cause of the distress. But many mothers in the 1950s were told by their own mothers and mothers-in-law to ignore the crying: 'Leave him to cry, he'll soon stop when he finds you don't come' or 'don't worry, he'll soon cry himself to sleep'; 'Start as you mean to go on and let him know who's the boss, if you don't, you'll be forever at his beck and call'; 'If you pick him up and cuddle him, he'll expect it all the time'. It was up to the mother to decide for herself how she was to treat this potential tyrant she had produced. Babies did not usually cry in their first weeks for no reason and it was necessary to pick them up to discover if they were hungry, needed changing or had acute wind. Once these had been either discounted or sorted, baby was likely to settle again. Could a quick cuddle to reassure him really hurt? Apparently so, according to some of the experts.

Bringing up a baby, it seemed, was all about training. Just as the owner of a puppy would make it a priority to house train it, so should the mother train her baby. According to Liddiard:

> 'Early training is of great importance; from the third day the nurse should have a small chamber [pot], a soap dish, or small pudding basin with a rounded edge on her knee, and the baby should be held with the back against the nurse's chest; the cold rim should just be allowed to touch the child at the back of the anus, and very soon a good habit is established. Many nurses train their babies so that they have no soiled nappies after the first week or so, and very few wet ones'.

Mrs Woodman obviously did not agree with this very early training, which might be possible when undertaken by trained nursery nurses but was difficult for young first-time mothers. Instead she tentatively suggests that sometime after the baby is 3 months old, the mother might make a note of the times when he was likely to soil his nappy and anticipate the times by placing him on a chamber pot. Eventually when a regular rhythm had been established, in a calm, matter-of-fact way, the baby would perform as required. On the whole Mrs Woodman thought proper training should not take place until the baby was old enough to sit up. So that was the time when many 1950s mothers began potty training. It seems to have been an issue that occupied many mothers' thoughts, almost turning the whole thing into a challenge the mother needed to win. One might occasionally overhear a young mother proudly telling another that she had got her child (usually a girl) clean before she was a year old. The implication behind this type of conversation was that the other mother was either negligent or a failure.

One wonders if some of this pressure to get their child out of nappies as quickly as possible had to do with the washing that was involved. The more relaxed attitude to toilet training that exists at the present time probably has more to do with the wide use of disposable nappies rather than the psychological impact it was thought to impose. Most 1950s mothers would have been horrified at the cost of modern disposables and certainly would not have been able to afford a weekly outlay on them. Instead they bought the terry towelling nappies in preparation for the baby and then accepted the work that was involved in dealing with dirty nappies. When calculating costs, most women expected to have more than one child, so the provision of two dozen terry towelling nappies and however many muslin ones that could be afforded – a long term investment. Amongst other essential equipment for dealing with nappies, not forgetting the two or three large safety pins, was the enamel pail with a lid. During the latter part of the 1950s the pail might have been made of plastic. When the baby was changed, a wet nappy was rinsed in cold water and then placed in a pail half-filled with mild soapy water until such time as it was washed. Soiled nappies were dealt with by flushing the contents into the WC pan and then rinsing them in the clean water as it refilled the pan. The nappy was then added to the pail, which probably contained a disinfecting fluid. Wet nappies could then be washed in hot soapy water – both Lux and Fairy soap flakes were in popular use. The stained ones, however, required boiling to get them really clean so many women simply boiled the whole lot.

Many houses still had shallow sinks with only a cold-water tap over it.

We have to remember that most 1950s kitchens were very different to the ones we have now. Many houses still had shallow sinks with only a cold-water tap over it. It was possible that if gas had been laid on in the house – and it was by no means standard – then an Ascot water heater might also be above the sink to provide limited amounts of hot water. If the house was old enough it might have a built-in copper in either a lean-to kitchen or outhouse. This would be filled from the kitchen tap or outside pump before lighting the fire under it to heat the washing water. Those who lived in the country unconnected to the mains water supply and sewage disposal often had no option but to heat their water in this way or in kettles and saucepans on the grate. Those who lived in houses that had gas or electric stoves often resorted to boiling up the nappies in another enamel bucket or a very large saucepan kept specifically for that purpose on the top of the stove. Lucky indeed were those who could afford an electric copper such as the Burco boiler, and luckiest of all were those who bought outright or on hire purchase an electric washing machine. These marvels not only heated the water to the correct temperature but also had a wringer attached to them. Unlike the modern, fully automated washing machines which include tumble drying, these early washing machines still required the housewife's participation in pumping out the washing water and refilling with clear water for rinsing. Nonetheless it was an improvement on hand washing and using a wringer on a stand, which occasionally showered the kitchen floor.

When the weather was fine, those who had access to an outdoor area would carry out the wet washing in a galvanised bath to where they had set up their wringer, or maybe even the old-fashioned mangle with its huge wooden rollers, and carefully pass each item through the wringer, placing each into a basket, ready to be pegged out on the washing line. Manufacturers of washing powders were quick to seize upon the importance of clean, white nappies, even producing advertisements of nothing more than a line full of white nappies against a beautiful blue sky. The housewife was not bombarded by adverts on television, since few homes had television sets in the early 1950s and the commercial channel had yet to be licensed. But wherever she went in towns and built-up areas she would be confronted with the huge billboards on which were displayed all the advertising material of the period. Imagine the pressure when, having just hung out a line full of nappies, on your walk to the shops you were dazzled by the brilliance of the images displayed by Persil, Oxydol or Omo.

Initially nappies and the cot bedding would have formed the major part of baby's laundry. Apart from boiling the soiled nappies, all his clothes would have required washing by hand. This was particularly so in the case of his woollen garments. All those lovingly knitted matinee jackets, bootees, bonnets and shawls needed delicate handling in warm water and soap flakes to make sure that they did not shrink. If the water was too hot, not only could shrinkage occur, but also, alas, the wool became matted and rough to the touch. Woollen items also required careful rinsing, had to be squeezed rather than wrung to remove excess water and then dried flat. All of this added to the work-load of the mother. How much easier life became with the introduction of synthetic materials that did not need such careful treatment.

The reader will recall that those giving advice to the mother-to-be encouraged her to take plenty of exercise in the fresh air. The new mother soon found that she was continuing to do this, though possibly not in the same way. The majority of women did not have help in the house, so once they had had their lying-in period of a maximum of two weeks, they were back to doing all the normal housework, cooking and shopping. No need for a gym to keep the 1950s housewife and mother fit, even if they had existed. The extra washing that the baby entailed meant that they exercised every part of their bodies, lifting pails, carrying out baskets of wet washing, wringing out washing if they did not pos-sess a wringer, or turning the handle of one if they did. They walked up and down the yard or garden to hang out the washing, often raising their arms to above head height as they pegged it out. No standing in one spot as one can nowadays to use a rotary clothes line. There was further exercise when all the washing was brought back into the house, where it was folded neatly ready for ironing. If it was still damp then it had to be put somewhere to air. This again needed the physical effort of putting it either on to the clothes dryer, consisting of several slats of wood fixed by a pulley system to the ceiling in the kitchen, or to the wooden clothes horse, which could be placed close to the living room fire, particularly at night. Not, however, a practice for those following the advice to put baby's cot in the living room at night. Miss Liddiard would not have approved of baby being left to sleep in a steamy atmosphere!

Several of the contributors report that it was the arrival of their baby that spurred them into the purchase of a washing machine; few would have been able to afford it outright so a hire-purchase (HP) agreement would have been entered into, often with the Electricity Board which had showrooms in most towns. A common comment from contributors was that they only took on one item at a time on HP, so perhaps they had paid off the cooker by the time they needed the washing machine. Some women, however, had doting parents who were in the position to give them the machine as a present – especially if the other grandparents had got in first with providing the baby's pram!

4

Baby's Carriage

Manufacturers of high-class perambulators in the 1950s referred to their products as 'baby carriages', harking back to the name that was given to them in Victorian times, when for the first time it became possible to transport an infant by mechanical means instead of carrying him. The earliest baby carriages made of basketwork resembled the small carriages often used by affluent ladies to take their daily airing, with a third wheel taking the place of a pony. But then came the heyday of British engineering, the growth of iron and steel works and the development of the railways and designs that infiltrated everyday life, even the baby carriage which now bore a distinct resemblance to the shape of the railway carriage of the period. Early twentieth-century prams had small wheels and a deep body set on springs. The interior was divided horizontally into three removable sections, on top of which was placed the mattress to accommodate the baby. To the modern eye these prams look ugly as well as very old-fashioned but they were very practical. Bearing in mind that many women gave birth to a second child within eighteen months of the first, with one of these prams she was able to remove the section in the middle and carry both children top to toe. These prams were sturdily built and lasted for years, often passing through several families.

However, they were not 'modern' or fashionable, and the 1950s mother, who may well have put her dolls in a miniature version of this particular carriage design, wanted something better for her baby. And at that time the name that everyone knew was Silver Cross; it could be said that a Silver Cross was the Rolls-Royce of prams. Surprisingly this comparison with cars had not escaped the manufacturers at Silver Cross who, in earlier times, had advertised their latest design beside the crème de la crème of motorcars. Queen Elizabeth and Princess Margaret were both wheeled out in a Silver Cross baby carriage. This then was the top status symbol and many new mothers aspired to own one for their little princess, or prince, as the case might be. Was it purely coincidental that many mothers commented that although their husbands played little part in baby's care in the early days, they had no objection to wheeling the pram? In fact some fathers even took the pram out by themselves, one wife reporting that her husband took the baby in the pram to the park on Sunday morning while she cooked the roast lunch for them and her parents in whose house they were living. However, a Silver Cross pram was expensive, well beyond the means of most, so the numbers of contributors who actually had a new one was small. Even second hand, like the Rolls-Royce, they demanded a high price.

On a very practical level was the advice given for what to look for when buying a pram. To start with the inside length should measure about 34in; the body should be made of wood or metal, the former being preferable; it should not be too deep but, alternatively, a pram that was too shallow was liable to tip up when the baby became active. It was important that prospective parents insisted on their pram having ball-bearing wheels and a brake. One can imagine that this bit of advice, very important though it was, was put in to appeal to the mechanical knowledge of the fathers-to-be, while for the mother, who would do most of the wheeling, there was the advice that the handle should be at a height that did not involve either stretching up or stooping forward. Further tips were given on how to look after the pram, ranging from general cleaning of the upholstery, examining regularly all the nuts and

The carriage-built perambulator that cost £17.

bolts, and oiling the hub and springs. When the pram had been out in the rain it was to be dried off thoroughly and the hood put up when not in use to prevent it from cracking. If the hood was made of leather then it could be cleaned with shoe polish or a wax floor polish. Any metal parts should be cleaned with a greasy rag while mud splatters were to be cleaned from the bodywork and caked mud removed from the wheels.

Some women felt very strongly that their baby should have everything new. Mrs W reported that when in 1950 a friend offered her a virtually unused Silver Cross she turned it down, insisting she wanted something new. Her Swan pram cost £17. At the time her husband was earning around £4 a week, so it was a long time before the hire-purchase loan was repaid and in the meantime economies had to be made on housekeeping. Most women preferred the popular high boat-shaped prams; they were easy to push and to manoeuvre, and the mother walked tall as she guided her pram. An additional advantage was that the baby was lying almost level with the mother's chest so from her end of the pram she could see the baby without having to bend down, and once the infant was sitting up facing her, they were in close eye contact and able to talk to each other. The biggest drawback to this type of pram was its size. In the early 1950s those who were living in rooms would probably not have had sufficient space in the house to accommodate a large pram. Films of the period often depict houses in multiple occupation where in order to get to the stairs it was necessary to negotiate from the front door past a pram as well as several bicycles. In many houses at that time the hall was very narrow so the pram had to be kept elsewhere. In those terrace houses where the front door opened straight into the front room, this became the obvious place for it, especially as the room was rarely used anyway. Suburban semi-detached villas that dated from the 1930s also lacked hall space but did boast quite a large dining room which again was probably only part furnished or rarely used except for special occasions. Actually, this room was ideal for following the advice given in the baby books, for this type of house would have had French windows that opened on to the garden. Thus, when the weather was too bad to put baby outdoors, the pram could be placed by the open garden doors.

However, the post-war house-building programme was still restricted by the shortage of materials. Building land was available but there were insufficient supplies of bricks and timber to meet the numbers of houses required for those who had lost their homes in the bombing as well as all the young couples, their number swelled by the marriages of returning servicemen. An attempt to alleviate some of the shortage came with the introduction of pre-fabricated bungalows. Built to fill the gap for up to twenty-five years, there are many estates throughout the country that, sixty years on, are still providing comfortable homes. But they were really not big enough to accommodate a large perambulator. When the new homes were being planned, few designers wasted valuable living space on large halls, so again there was no place for the pram. Eventually, the manufacturers of baby carriages got the message and by the end of the 1950s prams were becoming more compact; the high wheels gave way to smaller ones

> *When the pram had been out in the rain it was to be dried off thoroughly and the hood put up when not in use to prevent it from cracking.*

The small pram of the late 1950s.

supporting a much shallower body. A shortage of floor space, as much as the growing use of the car, has completely changed the way babies have been transported in the last forty years.

However, in the 1950s, regardless of what type of pram you had, your baby spent a great deal of time in it – and mainly outdoors. Two contributors volunteered the information that they put a carefully wrapped hot-water bottle in the pram when the weather was very cold, though neither professed to have read the books of the experts whom advocated this. Indeed one of them said the only advice she had received was from

her health visitor, so presumably it was standard practice. Baby was usually put outside, after his bath and
ten o'clock feed in the morning, in the expectation
that he would sleep until it was time for his next feed.
As he grew older and was able to sit up, the chances
were that the sleeping period would be shorter. When
this happened the infant was encouraged to play with
simple toys in his pram and to take notice of his surroundings. If he were in a garden then mother would
spare a few moments after she had sat him up, to point
out the flowers, the leaves on the trees, the singing of
the birds and so on, thus awakening his awareness of
the world around him.

The day would come, however, when the pram
had to be given up, perhaps to a new sibling or simply
because the baby was now a toddler and had become
too big for it. Colleen recalled:

> One really wet day when Mum wanted to go to the
> shops. My younger brother and I were both put in
> the Silver Cross pram, sitting side by side, with the
> hood up and the pram skirt on (the waterproof
> apron). We were 'parked' outside the newsagents'
> with strict instructions to wait, as Mum would not
> be long. We both sat there for a while but I decided
> 'she' had been long enough and I was going to find
> her, so I started climbing from under the hood to the
> handle end of the pram. My annoying little brother
> wouldn't wait on his own and decided he was
> coming too. That's when the pram tipped up, just as
> Mum came out of the shop ... She was cross with us!

Now was the time for the parents to buy the next mode
of transport, which rejoiced in the descriptive name of
a 'pushchair'. One cannot help wondering how long it

took the designers or manufacturers to come up with that. Was it, in fact, developed not from the pram at all but the high chair? With the skill and ingenuity of the late Victorian period, the straightforward wooden baby's chair had evolved so that parts could be folded down to make a low chair and, with the addition of small wheels incorporated into the design, the growing child had a chair in which he could push himself around. However it came about, this mode of transport was stuck with its name which is possibly more attractive than the current term of 'buggy', which harks right back to a single horse-drawn carriage, popular with young men in the early eighteenth century. The word was then taken to North America by English officers stationed there during the American War of Independence. But in the 1950s, pushchair it was. In the January 1951 edition of the magazine *Mother*, there is an item in the section titled 'Four O'clock Gossip' about the appointment of a new royal nursemaid, which is both interesting and relevant:

Baby was usually put outside, after his bath and ten o'clock feed in the morning, in the expectation that he would sleep until it was time for his next feed.

> Highlight of the junior Royal day remains the daily outing when Nurse Lightbody wheels out Princess Anne in the big black pram once used by Prince Charles. The two-year-old toddler – his new nursemaid thinks him a very lively and handsome boy – has now proudly graduated to a push-chair.

It would be interesting to know if 'the big black pram' was the same Silver Cross that had been delivered to the Duke and Duchess of York and used for both Queen Elizabeth and Princess Margaret.

The people of Suffolk, who have always been proud of their individuality and have in the past influenced the English language of the United States and Australia, promptly named the new pushchair a 'tripper', for the very simple reason that they could now take their toddlers on trips to places inaccessible with a pram. Colleen again:

> When the tripper was used my brother got to sit in it. The footplate used to raise and lock up so he could lay in it too when he was sleepy. If I got tired of walking I got to ride on the rear axle. If we both rode in it, he sat between my legs.

The wonderful thing about the pushchair was that compared with the pram they were smaller, lighter and, best of all, they could be folded up for stowage. The mother who had pushed her baby in its pram had been severely limited as to how far she could go. Although the 1950s women were more accustomed to walking than their modern counterparts, even those with the strongest legs would have found walking the 3 or 4 miles into the town centre from her home on a new housing estate a daunting prospect. But, with a pushchair, she could make use of the local trolley bus or tram. With the toddler either held secure on his reins or tucked under one arm, mother would release the mechanisms that collapsed the chair as the bus approached. In those days every bus had a conductor who collected the fares and was responsible for giving the signals to stop and start the bus. Most of them were ready to help a mother on board by taking the pushchair and placing it in the space on the platform under

the stairs, if it was a double-decker bus. When the
mother reached her desired stop, the conductor would
assist her by handing her the folded pushchair once
she had alighted. If he was not unduly busy and well
within his time schedule, conductors had been known
actually to help to the extent of reinstating the chair to
its normal position. Once she had reached the town-
centre shops, she was now able to take the baby in with
her; something that had previously been impossible
as few shops, for obvious reasons, would allow prams
to enter. Pram-pushers who did venture into town to
shop were forced to park their prams outside and either
carry the baby with them or risk leaving him outside.
A very new mother confessed that, having done that,
she completed her purchases, left the shop and was
about to enter another a little way further along the
street when she realised she had forgotten the pram.
Sixty years on and she shudders at the thought of what

This pushchair had been well used.

This was a newer model of pushchair.

might have been. At the time she was simply acutely embarrassed rather than concerned that harm might have come to the baby. But in the 1950s people were more trusting of each other.

This is borne out in another story that also fits in with the freedom that the pushchair gave. The whole travel scene was now opened up to young parents. The network of bus services throughout each county meant that it was possible to take your child on day trips to visit relations and friends in the country, for example. Similarly ,in summer time those who lived within reach of the coast were able to take advantage of bus or cheap day excursions by rail to the seaside. On this particular occasion a couple with a 1-2 year-old having a nap in the pushchair discovered that their other son, who was 2½, and minutes before had been happily digging in the sand beside their deckchairs, was nowhere to be seen. The beach was crowded and there were it seemed masses of little boys in knitted red swimming trunks and wearing white sun hats running around. The parents called his name and several little boys looked up but not theirs. Frantically father went off to search for him – but which direction had he taken? Mother scanned the sea in front of them, hardly daring even to consider the possibility he might have drowned. She felt helpless but she couldn't leave the other child, and then – there was the elderly gentleman who had their child by the hand. The man had been reading his newspaper when he saw the child, who incidentally was unperturbed by the whole episode, and realising he ought not to be alone, had led him safely back to his parents. This had all occurred within ten minutes yet it seemed like hours to the parents. It is a sad reflection on today's attitudes that a man in a similar situation might hesitate before helping. Once she had recovered from the shock, the mother was left thinking how much easier life had been when she had had him safely strapped in his big pram.

5

Customs, Practices and Old Wives' Tales

*I*n the 1940s at least 30 per cent of British boys were still being circumcised in the first few days after birth. However, once the operation was removed from the list of those covered by the new free National Health Service, the practice declined. It had risen in popularity in the early nineteenth century among the upper and middle classes when it was seen as a means of preventing sexually transmitted diseases. However, its use then became caught up in the austere moralistic attitudes of the latter part of the century that regarded masturbation as an unnatural vice, which would have disastrous effects on young boys, who were threatened that it would either make them blind or turn them into vicious, evil adults. It was believed that circumcision would combat all these unhealthy desires in youths. Probably ignoring the advice of her mother-in-law, who may have had her son circumcised as a matter of course in the 1930s, the average British mother of the 1950s would have been content to follow the advice of the health visitor or the instruction books and gently pulled her baby son's foreskin back during bath time. Miss Liddiard advised this should be done daily for the first month, then once a week for the next three months and thereafter monthly. Only if the foreskin was tight was it necessary for a doctor to be consulted. There is a slight whiff of the old-fashioned ideas in her remark that, on the whole, 'it is better to touch these organs as little as possible'.

However, there were, and still are, those for whom circumcision is part of their religious beliefs. Jewish boys are circumcised on the eighth day after birth. The ritual is performed by a specially trained member of the synagogue and is carried out either in the hospital or at home attended by close friends and family members. The baby is usually held for 'the operation' by his grandfather. Afterwards there is a family celebration. The ritual marks the entry of the child into the Jewish community and the receiving of his Hebrew name. Christians living in London and Manchester in particular during the 1950s would have been well aware that their Jewish neighbours did things slightly differently. But it is doubtful if they would have known much about the other religious group that practised circumcision both for strict hygienic reasons as well as religious ones. The terms 'Islam' and 'Muslim' were not part of the general vocabulary of the 1950s. They were then spoken of as Mohammedans, about whom very little was known.

The population as a whole in the 1950s professed itself to be Christian and as such there were religious practices that needed to be carried out once a baby was born. The first of these was the one known commonly

as the Churching of Women. The service as it appears in
the 1928 Book of Common Prayer was a Thanksgiving
of Women after Childbirth. It must have had its roots
in the ritual cleansing of women in biblical times. The
language, considered by some nowadays as old-fashioned, states in the rubric to the service: 'The woman,
at the usual time after her delivery, shall come into
Church, decently apparelled, and then kneel down
in some convenient place ... and then shall the priest
say unto her, "For as much as it hath pleased Almighty
God of his goodness to give you safe deliverance, and
hath preserved you in the great danger of child-birth:
You shall therefore give hearty thanks unto God and
say: Psalm 116".' There are parts of this Psalm that
must resound with every woman who has given birth
– and the archaic language reinforces those echoes:
'The snares of death compassed me round about; and
the pains of hell gat hold upon me. I found trouble
and heaviness, and I called upon the name of the Lord;
O Lord, I beseech thee, deliver my soul ... I was in
misery and He helped me.' What better description of
a woman in labour could you ask for than the 'pains
of hell gat hold'? Most of the women who contributed to this work who were members of the Church of
England said that they had been 'Churched'. As late as
1959, following the birth of her son, Mrs W 'attended
a Churching service in St Bartholomew's the Less, part
of the hospital and [also] received Holy Communion
from the priest at my bedside'. Another lady volunteered the information that someone she knew who
regularly attended the local Baptist church had, to her
surprise, attended a Churching at the local Anglican
church. This may have been a hangover from her early
upbringing in that church, the ritual being seen as both
a religious blessing and a good-luck symbol.

Rarely in the 1950s did the parents of a new baby adhere to another rubric that stated: 'that baby be baptized by the Second Sunday after birth.' It might in fact be several months before the baby was actually christened, though it was nicer if the child was still small enough to lie fairly still in the arms and fit into the family christening robe. This was often a beautifully made gown in fine white lawn material, the bodice inlaid with lace and possibly decorated with delicate embroidery. Often these gowns had been lovingly sewn by hand several generations earlier for the first of a family. After each wearing, it would have been carefully laundered and put away, wrapped in tissue paper. Eventually it would have been brought out for the first grandchild and so on down through the generations. Those in the 1950s who did not have heirlooms to use often started their own traditions, as Jean and

The christening robe that has become a family heirloom.

Jim, whom we mentioned earlier, did. In some families
the christening robe was accompanied by a very fine
knitted or crocheted shawl and a matching bonnet.
However, 1950s parents who considered themselves to
be modern and such things to be old-fashioned were
more likely to favour a pretty, frilly silk rayon dress for
their little girl and a smart romper suit for their son.
Whichever they chose, the likelihood was that the
yoke of both garments would have had smocking on
it, though that would have been done by a machine
rather than by hand. If the christening took place in
winter, then the dress or rompers would have been
covered with a matching set of knitted leggings, coat
and bonnet. Yes, baby boys wore bonnets too.

So much for the finery! The 1928 Book of Common
Prayer, which was used in church, specified that the
baptism should take place on a Sunday or holy day
when the greatest number of people were likely to
be present. This harked back to much earlier times,
before any form of written documents, when it was
essential that there were as many witnesses as possible able to testify that the child had in fact been born
and baptised. It was also symbolic: the congregation
was receiving the child into the church but, at the same
time, each member of the congregation was reminded
of the religious promises that had been made at their
own baptisms. So the actual baptism formed part of the
service known as Morning Prayer or Evening Prayer,
which in fact would have been in the afternoon. The
usual service would have carried on until after the
reading of the second lesson, at which point the priest
would go to the font at the back of the church, around
which had gathered the parents and baby and the godparents – two godfathers and a godmother for a boy
and two godmothers and a godfather for a girl. Other

family and friends would remain in their pews or seats. The actual baptismal service was quite lengthy and it was the mother's fervent hope that the baby would remain asleep for most of it – another reason to have the service while the baby was still fairly tiny. Once a baby was at the sitting-up stage it was likely to take notice of what was happening and to object vigorously to the priest taking it and sprinkling the holy water from the font and making the sign of the cross on its forehead as he named the child. If the child cried at this point, the 'old wives' could breathe a sigh of relief. It was a sign: the cry denoted the devil was leaving the child.

In some parish churches it was more convenient to hold a specially designed communal baptismal service for several babies on a Sunday afternoon. This was popular with couples whose friends had young children of their own whom they could bring with them. Sunday afternoon was often better for catering for the christening party that followed. A morning baptism meant providing guests with a lunch of some sort while tea and cakes was quite acceptable for the afternoon. Whether it was a large family celebration or a small gathering with a few friends, christening cake would have been regarded as essential. Traditionally the top tier of a rich fruit wedding cake was reserved for the first baby's christening. This recalled the days when the wedding cake was laced with alcohol that acted as a preservative, and it was also taken for granted that a baby would arrive by the time the first wedding anniversary arrived. Many couples did in fact keep their top tier wrapped in greaseproof paper in an airtight tin. However, many were also disappointed to discover, when they came to look at it, that the white icing had discoloured. Enterprising mothers might remove the icing and marzipan thinking they could re-ice the cake only to find that the cake itself had gone mouldy. Better to discover that than to take trouble redecorating it and then serve a dry, unpleasant-tasting cake.

The christening was also the time to bestow gifts upon the child. Remember the story of Sleeping Beauty? All the fairies who were invited to her christening endowed her with virtues to guide her through life – except the wicked fairy who had not received an official invitation and so cursed the child. Was there a warning in this ancient story that parents should choose the child's godparents wisely and that they should make sure they did not offend anyone by omission? Traditionally godparents gave items made of silver, both as a symbol of future wealth and as something the child might fall back on in time of need. The silver christening mug or cup dates back hundreds of years; the 1950s' offering was more likely to be EPNS (Electro Plated Nickel Silver) and spent its life in a display cabinet along with the tablenapkin ring and photograph frame. Other popular gifts then were little cutlery sets designed for when the baby started eating proper food; these could be silver or stainless steel with ceramic handles painted with nursery figures. Little girls were likely to be given tiny silver bangles to wear while they were small, charm bracelets or silver crosses and chains to be worn when they were much older. One of these or an ivory-backed prayer book was often given by the godmother. Prudent relations might give National Savings Certificates in the child's name, which invested a sum of money for a certain term of years; a most useful financial start for the child and an encouragement as they grew older to save birthday and Christmas money gifts.

Before we have a frivolous look at old wives' tales, there are one or two practices relating to children that were still in operation in the early 1950s. Of these, the one that had the most long-lasting effect was forcing a naturally left-handed child to use its right. Mothers must have noticed fairly early if their child indulged in those other 'bad habits' of thumb-sucking or hair-twiddling using their left hand. The inclination to the left became more apparent once the child tried to feed itself, whether it was a question of holding a rusk, a cup or a spoon. Many mothers tried to enforce the use of the right hand, while others simply left the child to develop as he wished. This was fine but, when the time came for school, there were still teachers of the old school of thought, who would insist that the child must learn to write with his right hand. There were stories such as that of the very strict teacher who actually tied the child's left hand behind his back, forcing him to use the other. The psychological damage this practice caused was only just being recognised in the 1950s, but generations of children had suffered the ignominy of being labelled 'different' and having to learn to perform actions that to them seemed totally unnatural. There are still those who, having been 'corrected', will write with their right hand and hold cutlery in the conventional manner but draw and paint, throw balls and darts, and so on, with their left. There are even those who can cleverly write with both hands at the same time, producing an entertaining trick of mirror glass writing.

> *Traditionally godparents gave items made of silver, both as a symbol of future wealth and as something the child might fall back on in time of need.*

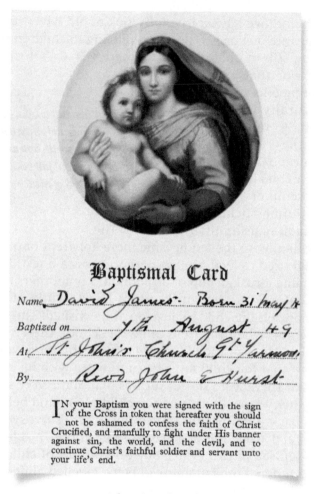

A baptismal card.

There had been a time in the past when as soon as a mother had seen her tiny baby sucking its thumb she would have congratulated herself that she had a good baby, one that was able to suck strongly and therefore likely to thrive. However, as we know, ideas and fashions change and in the 1930s thumb- or finger-sucking was severely frowned upon. Apparently in the 1930s thumb sucking increased, thought to be due to a similar increase in bottle-feeding. Apparently thumb-sucking became a form of compensation but unfortunately many fathers, in particular, were so appalled to see a toddler thumb-sucking that various expedients were tried to cure the habit. These included putting the child's offending hand into an elbow splint, thus pre-

it had become the practice to increase the size of the hole in the bottle's teat, thus making it unnecessary for the baby to have to make the effort to suck.

venting the thumb from being put into the mouth, bandaging the hand or painting the thumb and fingers with foul-tasting concoctions, the best known of which was bitter aloes. This surely was 'aversion therapy' before the modern term was coined.

We may laugh now at the comment in *The Mothercraft Manual*: 'that thumb sucking is now regarded in the same way as masturbation, and when it is not pernicious need not be dealt with.' The manual was talking about the habit forming in the very early days and advised that the best ways of tackling it were for the baby to wear cotton gloves or to have its arms tightly tucked down with the bed-clothes: 'The prevention of a bad habit being formed is preferable to the subsequent cure.' As far as the writer of the manual was concerned: 'It is very unlikely that a baby who is having the right food, enough mothering and all the other essentials mentioned in this book will develop the habit perniciously.' It is words like pernicious, which is defined in the dictionary as 'destructive, ruinous, fatal', that set thinking in the manual firmly in an earlier era than the 1950s even though it was still in general use. In fact, even in the late 1960s a retired district nurse, a grand-mother, advised that her daughter-in-law should paint her 2-year-old son's thumb with bitter aloes. This same remedy was also recommended to stop a child biting its fingernails.

Fortunately, the more modern thinking of the 1950s was that thumb-sucking was quite normal. In fact it started in the womb. If it continued as the child grew, then that too was natural; the child would eventually grow out of it by the time he was 3. Most frequently it was a sign of tiredness and used by the child to lull itself to sleep. During the day it could be a sign of boredom, so then it was time for mother to step in and divert the child's attention. Certainly, the last thing the child needed was to have someone con-tinually drawing attention to the habit, for that could cause tension and make things worse. Of course, mothers had to bear with those well-meaning friends who muttered strongly that the child's teeth would grow crooked or protrude.

Where thumb-sucking could perhaps be put down to a fault in the baby, with the use of a dummy, which was definitely frowned upon in the 1950s and into the 1960s, it was without doubt the result of the mother's inadequacy. If she had trained her baby properly from birth, making sure that it was receiv-ing the correct amount of sustenance and was clean and dry, then there was no need for this appalling item to be inserted into the baby's mouth. If the baby cried, then that was mother's fault and she should not pander to the child by giving it a dummy or pacifier, as it was sometimes known. The use or not was often a great bone of contention between a young mother and the child's grandmothers, who would issue dire warnings as to the harm that would be done to the development of the child's mouth and teeth.

If you wanted to ensure that your child did not have bowed legs, then on no account should a baby who was not ready to walk be allowed to put its feet to the ground while being held.

It is possible to understand the fear of germs being introduced, especially when the dummy has been dropped on the ground, given a quick wipe and then put back in the infant's mouth. It is interesting to note that the once forbidden object, which caused so many women to feel great guilt if they yielded to its use, is now known as what it is, a comforter.

Superstitions and old wives' tales are fast disappearing; those that remain are treated with levity. No one today hesitates to hold a baby in front of a mirror to see himself – in fact it is often a useful distraction for a grizzling infant to see what his face looks like. In the past it was believed that to do so would cause the child to cut its teeth on the cross, whatever that meant. Mrs L obviously did not believe such superstitious rubbish as she noted in her record that at 19 weeks old her little girl 'likes to see her reflection in the mirror, makes a mess of the mirror though'. Miss Liddiard believed that objects dangling above the child in its pram or cot could make it too excitable, whilst the old wives foretold the baby's eyes would suffer, causing a squint. If you wanted to ensure that your child did not have bowed legs, then on no account should a baby who was not ready to walk be allowed to put its feet to the ground while being held.

Indigestion often accompanied the later stages of pregnancy so frequent bouts of heartburn were put down to the coming child having either a lot of hair or perhaps curly hair. In these days of antenatal scans which can show the sex of the unborn child, there is no longer any reason to listen to those who would insist that the pregnant woman who appeared to be carrying high would produce a girl but for the one whose extra weight was all around it would be a boy. There was another idea that the woman who craved sweet things would have a girl while cravings for sour things indicated a boy. This actually fits in with the nursery rhyme 'what are little girls made of? Sugar and spice and everything nice', little boys, however, were made of 'snips and snails and puppy dogs' tails'– in other words the more unusual, that is sour, items. In the 1950s there was no way of knowing what sex your child would be, so the curious resorted to the old wives' practice of dangling a wedding ring suspended from a thread of cotton – the old wives were supposed to have used a strong hair from the woman's head – above the expectant mother's tummy. Rather like dowsing for water with a hazel twig that twists violently when water is detected, the ring either swung from side to side, indicating a boy, or went round in circles for a girl. The author confesses that, one afternoon, to relieve the boredom for a ward of some ten women who were incarcerated in a maternity hospital for several weeks because of various pre natal problems, she applied this test. Much hilarity ensued, followed by a severe reprimand from the ward sister when it was discovered that everyone's blood pressure readings had gone up. Perhaps after all it is best to leave superstitions alone.

6

Baby's First Year

What amazing progress a baby makes in the first twelve months of his life; probably more than he will ever make again. It is mind-blowing when you stop to think about it. What starts as a tiny, perfectly formed miniature human being incapable of doing anything for himself, 365 days later has learned to sit up, grow teeth, exchanged an all-milk diet for mixed feeding and can recognise not only family members but also others he sees regularly. He has become mobile: crawling, standing upright, holding on to things, he tries to climb, he may even be walking unaided by the end of the year. He is beginning to talk and has probably already, to his mother's disappointment, said 'Dada' rather than 'Mama'! He readily responds to language, delighting in complying with such requests as 'wave goodbye'.

The *Sunday Express Baby Book* besides offering so much useful information, also gave new parents the opportunity to keep a 'Record Section of Your Child's Physical and Mental Growth, Personality, Interests and Abilities'. In the introduction to this section it was emphasised that keeping such records was much more than mere sentiment: doctors were asking mothers to note down, somewhere safe, details of their child's physical development, so that in the future any physicians who might have to care for them could refer back to constitutional problems or acquired susceptibilities. Thus by keeping these details, all parents were contributing towards scientific research into general health problems. If that was not exciting enough a challenge, then on an individual basis, these notes might one day interest not only members of the medical profession but also be a guide 'to vocational counsellors in high school or college days'. They might even help the parents towards a better understanding of each of their children as well as being a source of pleasure for years to come. The time might come when the grandchildren had arrived, and the new generation of parents were bewailing their offspring's inability to sleep or their 'naughtiness', when production of the record book could remind them of what they had been like!

Since breast and cows' milk both lack iron, by the time it is about four months, a baby will have exhausted its natural store and is in danger of becoming anæmic.

Mrs L was meticulous in her record keeping which started with the first few days from birth and concentrated on any problems associated with breast- or bottle-feeding. The next two-week period dealt with establishing a routine at home, beginning with the first night at home, assuming the birth had taken place in hospital or a nursing home. By the time Mrs L had spent ten days in the nursing home in February/March 1951, her daughter had already 'been trained' by the staff, so the note for her first night at home reads: 'Slept through from 11 pm until 6 am.' However, twenty-one months later, having come home with a 4-day-old son, it was a different story: 'A's first night at home wasn't too good, but afterwards was very good, although he wakened for a 2 am feed.' One has to admire the painstaking diligence with which over the next four days Mrs L carefully filled in the required information: 'Wakened: Had feed; Slept from … to …; Cried from … to …; Bath and feed; Slept from … to …; and so on throughout the day – and night. It has to be said that these details were given only for the first baby. At the end of four weeks Mrs L commented on the baby's routine. Of her daughter she wrote: 'She is sleeping in her own room and doesn't waken after 10 pm feed until 6 am. Is good during the day but has to have a play time about 4 pm after her walk.' The editor of the *Sunday Express Baby Book* would have been proud of her: she was following all the guidance she had been given and had produced a textbook baby. Not so with baby number two: 'He doesn't seem at all settled. He doesn't sleep well between feeds and wakens for his 2 am feed although he is gaining well.' However where her little girl had disliked her

'The true meaning of the term 'to wean' is to accustom the child to other foods, but it does not mean that the baby is being taken off the breast, or the bottle.'

dose of cod liver oil, her son happily took both and
wanted more of the orange juice!

The next section covered from six weeks to four
months and began with a chart in which to record the
baby's weekly weight, plus space to note when the
child was vaccinated. The little girl received her smallpox vaccination at 18 weeks while the little boy had his
at 14 weeks. On the next page but one after the chart
appeared the heading 'Illnesses' with the injunction
to,'Describe symptoms, severity and duration of attack
and treatment.' As if Mrs L, with two small children,
did not have enough to contend with:

> A's vaccination upset him rather, he had quite a
> temperature and was unwell for 3 days. The skin
> around the original vaccination inoculated itself &
> he had about 10 more blisters also a rash and one
> other blister on his chest. All this cleared within
> a week.

On the second half of this page, under the heading
'Special Problems', Mrs L confided:

> A wasn't very good in the night till he was 14 weeks.
> He slept from 6 pm to 1 or 2 and then till 6 am. After
> feeding him at 10 one night and leaving him to cry,
> he sorted himself out and slept from 11 to 5.30.
> At 15 weeks has been very good all day and much
> better at night.

'Have you started weaning him yet?' This was the question most asked by anxious grannies after 'have you
started potty training?' *The Handbook for Nursery Nurses*,
published in 1947, gives its readers the definition of
this much bandied around word: 'The true meaning of

the term *"to wean"* is to *accustom the child to other foods,* but it does not mean that the baby is being taken off the breast, or the bottle.' We are then given the information that the baby is born with a store of iron obtained from its mother during the latter months of pregnancy. This was why expectant mothers were issued with iron tablets along with their vitamins. Since breast and cows' milk both lack iron, by the time it is about 4 months old, a baby will have exhausted its natural store and is in danger of becoming anaemic. Thus it became necessary to start providing fresh fruit and vegetables, liver and the yolk of eggs to supply those necessary minerals and vitamins. All these had to be sieved or pulped or finely mashed and introduced to the baby by the half teaspoonful to begin with at the 2 p.m. feed. Suggested for the first week were sieved purées of vegetables such as spinach, cabbage, carrots and swedes with a little bone or marmite gravy. That suggests that the mother was a good housewife who made her own stock from bones. Alternatively she might feed her infant half a teaspoonful of steamed brains. (Do butchers these days actually have brains for sale?) By the second and third week after beginning the weaning process, baby was being given a hard baked crust spread with butter at 10 a.m., with steamed fish being introduced at 2 p.m. At 6 p.m. came another buttered crust or rusk. In the fourth and fifth week porridge or yolk of egg on toast or rusk alternated with bread and butter spread with the pulp of fresh fruit such as apple, banana or orange in the morning. Every fortnight following, the child's range of foods was widened and the amounts increased, but always the emphasis was on the preparation of freshly cooked fresh foods.

Like so much of the advice in the books of the period, opinions differed as to when different processes should take place. For example, Nestlé's *You and Your Baby*, recommends starting at 4 months old with half to one tablespoonful of bone and vegetable broth, alternating with meat and vegetable broth and liver and tomato soup. At 5 months we progress to half to two teaspoonsful of yolk of egg or groats made with milk at 10 a.m., puréed carrots as well as vegetable or liver soup at 2 p.m., while at 6 p.m.the child is offered 2oz of baby cereal with milk. The breast or the bottle is still given at each feed. On the other hand, Miss Liddiard advised that the ideal feeding programme for baby was to continue to breast feed totally for nine months and then take five weeks over weaning, by which time the child would be completely off the breast. This did not mean that she did not introduce solids into the baby's diet. She advocated vegetable purées of pulped spinach, lettuce and raisins at 6 months, while at 7, the baby should be given a hard baked crust of bread cut into fingers. The baby, we are told, should not be allowed to play with this but, seated on mother's knee, should have the crust held in its mouth until it learnt to suck on it. Within days it will become a treat, she said. She warned against the crusts being crisp instead of hard and the danger of leaving the baby alone with it. And then came a further warning that sounds as if it was issued today: 'Baked crusts are preferable to the much-advertised rusks for two reasons: a) They are not sweet; a child who is accustomed to always have something sweet to suck will want everything he takes sweetened, and so get much too high a percentage of carbohydrate in his diet. b) Rusks melt in the mouth just being sucked while the bread needs masticating.' With remarks such as this, one imagines that Miss Liddiard was not popular with Farleys, manufacturers of commercial rusks. Realistically not every mother had time to bake crusts of bread when she could buy them in a packet. Undeterred, Liddiard continued to give her recommendations, all of them very nutritious but boring by modern standards: at 8 months old, for example, the child should be started on a tablespoonful of sieved porridge twice a day, the amount being increased to three tablespoons by the time the child was a year. It also should be noted that not all the books agreed on the subject of sweetening; for example the Nestlé book when talking about the importance of giving baby cod or halibut liver oil daily and including two teaspoonsful of orange, tomato, rosehip or blackcurrant juice adds: 'this should be diluted in water, and sugar to sweeten, if necessary'.

For the sieved porridge mentioned above, many mothers substituted the manufactured cereal, Farex. Mrs L's son was introduced to this in his 6 p.m. feed at 13 weeks old and began having broth at 15 weeks. His sister had teaspoons of chicken broth and bone and vegetable broth, the latter being much preferred, from 3½ months, but within four weeks she was insisting that she drank her soup straight from the cup. At 17 weeks she was introduced to a hard-boiled egg mashed with boiled milk; she loved it so much that Mrs L had to ration her to seven teaspoons at a meal. Also at this time, she was introduced to Scotts' cereal oats, mixed with boiled milk and sweetened. Her mother wrote: 'She loved it – ate the lot.' The following week she had discovered a new game: blowing bubbles in the spoon as she was being fed. Her mother thought she liked the noise it made. Both of Mrs L's children were given their first taste of chocolate at around 18 weeks. The little girl loved it and cried for more.

We tend to think the interest in the way celebrities do things is a recent phenomenon but this is not so. Although the emphasis nowadays is likely to be focused upon pop stars, footballers' wives and TV personalities, the 1950s magazines were not averse to giving their readers interesting details of those whose lives were very far removed from the average woman. Many new young mothers, faithfully following the specialist books, must have been shaken by the article that appeared in that first issue of *Mother and Baby* in January 1956. Entitled 'How I am bringing up my Baby', Mrs T, 'the beautiful young daughter of a baronet, describes her routine for M aged five months'. The 20-year-old mother told the magazine that although her son had been born in a London nursing home, she believed it was preferable – and cheaper – to have the baby at home, unless there were complications, as there had been in her case with her son having being a breech presentation. However, it was what Mrs T had to say on feeding that might have shaken other mothers. She was able to feed her baby herself, so successfully that he was in fact overfed. To cut his weight gain he was put on to neat cows' milk at 3 months, having already started cereals once a day at 2 months! Mrs T's unusual approach continued and at 5 months the baby was fed as late as possible at night, usually at 11.30 p.m. He was given orange juice at 8 a.m. and his first feed of the day at 10 a.m., which included cereal. The magazine commented: 'Mothers who follow a more orthodox routine of feeding will no doubt be astonished to know that M has canned sieved vegetables and fruit or an egg for lunch. His

'It is good for Baby to see some outside people, but his eating and sleeping routine should on no account be disturbed.'

mother plans to give him grated cheese and fish in the near future. If baby needs a laxative at any time, Mrs T substitutes brown sugar for white in his feed. This, she assured us, always works.' As if this wasn't enough to have many of the establishment reeling, there was more to come in the revelation that Mrs T disliked the idea of a boy in long clothes, so he had been put in rompers from birth. Her only concession was the use of a nightgown for him since she could not find pyjamas small enough. Then there was the attitude of both parents that they should not cut back on their evenings out, for as Mrs T pointed out, as the baby was asleep he would not see his parents anyway. Of course Mrs T did employ a Spanish nanny but she assured the magazine interviewer that even if she could not afford a nanny, she would prevail upon friends and relations to babysit since she thought it vitally important to the success of a marriage that husband and wife should be able to go out together as often as possible. Mr T, it seemed, had his own infallible method of stopping the baby crying by dancing with him to the music of the hottest jazz. The interviewer, in recognising that the Ts had shattered several old-fashioned notions, wondered if the couple's realism might be more successful than the 'woolly-minded idea that to be a good mother one must sit at home, patiently, while baby sleeps his head off, oblivious of the sacrifices being made for him'. It would have been interesting to know what the general reaction to Mrs T's account was. Were there thousands of women cheering her on and deciding to take a leaf out of her book, while others looked disapproving, and bewailed the attitudes of the modern generation? For any reader who is interested, research reveals that after having another son and a daughter, the Ts were divorced within ten years.

In contrast, the Ls are still living happily together after more than sixty years so we return to look at the entries in Mrs L's *Sunday Express Baby Book*. The next record page covered the period from 6-12 months and contained not only spaces for each month's weight but also those for the appearance of the first six teeth. That children develop at different rates is clearly shown in the comparison between Mrs L's four children. Their first tooth appeared at 13½ weeks, 17, 20 and 20½ respectively, yet they each had all six by 33 weeks. Interestingly, the two boys cut their teeth first. All four were sitting up alone at 24 weeks and began crawling around 32 to 36 weeks. Between 28 and 36 weeks they all came out with their first words – Da-Da-Da! Is this sound the result of nature preparing the child's back gums ready for teeth or is it because mother talks to the child about daddy?

Every period in a baby's development is exciting for its parents but there is so much excitement for all of them once the baby is sitting up and taking notice. From around 6 months all sorts of changes can be made, for example bathing in the big bath. Some of the advice the editor gives in the *Sunday Express Baby Book* now seems very dated and it is doubtful if many mothers followed it to the letter. Under the heading 'He gets a Social Life', she writes: 'It is good for Baby to see some outside people, but his eating and sleeping routine should on no account be disturbed. He can go visiting occasionally between 3 o'clock and bedtime.' That last sentence sounds almost as if it might have appeared as etiquette for infants in Mrs Gaskell's *Cranford*. Worse

Having established that the baby was sleeping less during the day, the playpen came into its own.

was to follow: 'visitors may play with him quietly during that period. He should not be tossed, tickled, spoken to loudly, or made to laugh hard. These things are over-stimulating, and most babies pay for them with crying spells.' Oh dear, oh dear, how could one explain to grandpa that he mustn't toss the baby in the air, especially if the baby giggles when he does so? Leave it to grandma, she will tell him if she thinks it necessary. On the whole, one cannot help feeling that the baby was, to a certain extent, to be excluded from all company even though the editor does suggest 'it is nice for baby to join the family circle while eating his rusk and for a time before the evening meal'. However, the editor's main concern over baby's mixing with people was fear of infection. 'People, not draughts or cold air, give colds to babies. People also give them children's and other diseases. Do not let anyone with an infection near your baby.' One might now be tempted to say, 'bless you, dear Mrs Woodman, but most of us live in the real world and have to take it as it is.' And, of course, that was exactly what most mothers did.

On the other hand, there was down-to-earth advice on what baby should now be wearing. Although his vest and nappy remained the basic requirements, once the baby was moving around on the floor and outside when the weather was warm, then the knitted suits and dresses could be replaced with what were referred to at that time as overalls, or later as dungarees. Made of cotton that was both hardwearing and washable, these all-in-one garments were ideal, especially if the legs were fastened with press-studs, which made nappy-changing easier. Having established that the baby was sleeping less during the day, the playpen came into its own. Mothers were advised to put this outside as much as possible either on a sheltered porch or on the grass if the weather was really warm, making sure that the area was also shaded and there was a rug in the bottom of the playpen. Here the baby could be left to amuse himself with his rattle and soft cloth or knitted toys and perhaps a soft ball. During inclement weather the playpen could be used in the house. Wherever it was placed, play time for baby was when mother got on with her housework. We know, even if the writers of the period did not mention it, that there were huge numbers of women who lived in cramped surround-ings without access to sheltered porches or gardens with grass. Those who lived in those high-rise 1950s blocks of flats certainly did not, though some did have a balcony of sorts where they hung their washing out to dry. Alternatively, those who lived in high-density terraced housing with a communal courtyard would have been able perhaps to park a pram outside either the front or back door, but certainly not a playpen.

The advantage of the pen was that once the baby had started to crawl, the next stage in his development was to pull himself up to the standing position. The sturdy old style wooden playpen gave him plenty of support for this. The more modern models made of tubular steel and mesh with a fitted floor did not perhaps give the child quite so much scope for inventive-ness. As he became really strong, many, having found their feet as it were, discov-ered they could push against the bottom rail

As the baby is allowed more freedom to crawl outside the playpen, then certain objects come within his reach on coffee tables and low shelves.

and move the whole thing. Wonderful fun, not entirely appreciated when it crashed into something precious. An event like that brings us to the major decision every mother has to make, or as Mrs Woodman had it, 'your first great problem of management'. As the baby is allowed more freedom to crawl outside the playpen, certain objects then come within his reach on coffee tables and low shelves. The dilemma was, do you remove the precious items or those that might damage the child in some way, or do you teach your child not to touch? One school of thought was that a baby cannot be expected

Alas, today's meat joints rarely provide sufficient fat to make dripping.

to ignore things within reach, but as it was all part of a phase that would pass, you should simply remove temptation. Others maintained, as did our editor, that it was perfectly possible to teach baby to leave your things alone. It was, naturally, common sense to remove irreplaceable objects out of reach but it was also well worth spending time training baby in the way she advocated. This was to be done by constantly watching baby as he crawled around freely, and when he picked up something you were to say pleasantly, '"That is Mother's". As you take the object from him, give him an object he may have in exchange, saying, "This is baby's". Replace the forbidden object and be at hand to do this whenever the need arises'. Apparently this method, which required constant and patient work for a week or more, would succeed. Unfortunately, the question 'Did you remove precious objects or train your baby not to touch?' was not one that was asked of my 1950s mothers. Had it been, I suspect that the answer might have been, 'we didn't have any breakable objects within child reach', for as we have already established most of the decade was still feeling the effects of austerity and small salaries so left little room for expensive decorative items. On the other hand, it was sensible never to leave cups of tea or ash trays unattended on low coffee tables while patiently persevering to teach your infant that they did not touch these.

By now our baby has reached 10 months and is ready to have three meals a day. The Nestlé book offers the following menu, which demonstrates how times have changed since the 1950s. We are to assume that mother and father are having a cooked breakfast of bacon and eggs. For baby it is recommended that he has bread fried in bacon fat or dripping or a buttered crust. Three times a week he may have half a lightly boiled egg, with groats or barley kernels with milk on the other days. There may be readers who have no idea what dripping is, or perhaps was, is better. Although the Sunday joint was not large, the meat, unlike joints today, was usually sold with its natural fat on it. When placed in the oven a small quantity of lard was put on top to keep the meat moist. After cooking, the joint was removed from the cooking pan and some of the juices were poured off to make gravy. Those that remained were placed in a small, clean basin and allowed to cool. Eventually the fat would rise to the surface and solidify, while underneath would be the most delicious meaty jelly. That spread on hot toast or just a slice of bread was considered a real treat, especially in winter. The fat on top was known as dripping and was used for frying eggs or bread. Alas, today's meat joints rarely provide sufficient fat to make dripping. The recommendation for baby was that he should have his fried bread made using bacon fat. Again it is a sign of the times that most of the bacon we now buy contains so much preservative and water that it is impossible to use it to make fried bread. And, of course, nowadays we are told that fried foods are not good for us anyway.

Lunch for baby could be drawn from whatever the parents were having. In the quoted menu this consists of minced meat (possibly the remains of the Sunday joint), rabbit or tripe with potatoes and mashed vegetables. If the parents were not eating, then the child could have one of the homogenised broths, bone and vegetable or meat and vegetable; or a coddled egg (not, we assume, on one of the days when egg was taken at breakfast, nor is it made clear if this counted as one of the three weekly) with potatoes and vegetable marrow; or broth and coddled yolk of egg and breadcrumbs; or steamed fish such as herrings or broth and fish pudding. This was followed by a milk pudding made from ground rice, semolina or cornflour, or a baked apple and custard or a sponge pudding. Baby could drink water with this meal. Between four and five o'clock baby would have his tea/supper, which consisted of either a buttered crust or bread and butter spread with seedless jam or honey, or Marmite sandwiches. The meal finished with some plain cake and milk to drink. Finally he would have another small drink of milk before he went to bed. Mothers following these menus were reminded that it was still necessary for baby to have his cod liver oil and fruit juice during the day. By the time he was a year old baby had graduated to eating half a rasher of bacon for breakfast – many mothers would give their baby the crisp rind with the fat attached to suck. He might also have toast and dripping. For lunch there were lots of mashed

> *The most usual variety on sale was called honeycomb tripe and can best be described as somewhat resembling a new hand-knitted dishcloth.*

vegetables to accompany stewed tripe, steamed brains or sweetbreads, while in summer salads with grated cheese were introduced. Puddings included steamed sponge or suet with fruit or junkets, and fruit such as stewed apple and blackcurrant juice. Tea brought sandwiches with different fillings: Marmite, grated cheese, chopped mustard and cress, jam and honey. At the end of these suggested menus comes the warning: 'ill chosen-meals can be the forerunners of future trouble and it is, therefore, a good policy to pay special attention to the diet during the early years of life.'

Some readers may have no knowledge of the delicacy called tripe, which appears so often in these menus. It comes under the heading of offal and is part of the stomach lining in cows, pigs or oxen. What is sold in shops has been bleached and partially cooked. The most usual variety on sale was called honeycomb tripe and can best be described as somewhat resembling a new hand-knitted dishcloth. It is said the tripe from the ox has the best flavour. The following is a recipe that appeared under the heading of 'Nursery Recipes' in *Mother and Baby* magazine:

Ingredients: 1 lb. Tripe; 6 onions; 3 carrots; 1 oz butter; 1 pint stock; ½ pint milk; Pepper and salt.
Method: (Tripe cooked this way may be included in a baby's diet from the age of one year.) Melt the butter in a casserole. Slice the carrots and onions and fry them in the butter until brown. Cut the tripe into small pieces about 2 inches square; add it to the onions and carrots in the casserole with salt and pepper to taste; stir in the stock and milk. Cover closely and cook either in a slow oven or over a low gas for four or five hours.

The child who had that for his first course would probably find that for pudding he had a semolina cream
– another way of making sure he had plenty of milk
– or perhaps, as a special treat, a baked rice pudding
which, having spent two hours in a slow oven, would
have developed the thick skin on the top which was
either loved or detested by the children of the 1950s.
Although tripe may have disappeared from his menu
once the baby was able to join the family for all his
meals, his diet would not have changed radically. The
'1950s children's' recollection is of home-made meat
pies and puddings, carrots, sprouts, peas and cabbage
followed by more puddings and pies with custard.
One should find it amazing that all over the country
families were producing similar dishes day in day out,
until we remember that the country was still suffering
from limited supplies of some foods while others were
beyond the price range of many. On the whole the
English were very conservative about what they ate: a
roast dinner on Sundays, with cold meat, mince, sau-
sages and stewing beef accompanied by potatoes and
a vegetable throughout the rest of the week, always
followed by a dessert of some sort. The 1950s babies
would have to wait until they reached the 1970s before
their habits would change enough to allow them to
give dinner parties at home or go out to a restaurant
to enjoy the three-course favourite of prawn cocktail,
steak and chips and Black Forest gateau.

7

Brothers, Sisters and Friends

*D*uring the 1950s the flocks of storks flying over the United Kingdom must have been tremendous judging by the rapid increase in the birth rate! Most contributors reported that they had their second child within eighteen months to two and a half years of the first. One lady commented when describing the small gap between her two sons 'we were very naïve (ignorant?)'. In those pre-contraceptive pill days, many young married women expected their husbands to 'take the precautions', which unfortunately did not always prove to be a 100 per cent reliable. So often it was not until after the arrival of the second child that the wife sought advice from the Family Planning Clinic. The couple were then faced with the choice of the husband continuing to use condoms or the wife being fitted with one of the intrauterine devices. Although the contraceptive pill was being tested towards the end of the 1950s it was not readily available, or in use, until the 1960s.

However, there were those who were keen to have a second child, since in those early years of the 1950s the number of children in the family increased the chances of being allocated a council house. Often a couple with one child might have to share half a house with another small family, but once the second child was expected it was likely that the family would be given priority for a whole house as soon as one became available. Other couples, who were already settled and perhaps had to put off starting a family for financial reasons, decided that, having got one child, they might as well have another as soon as possible. There was even a belief among some women that if they were having to wash one lot of nappies, they might as well wash two and get it over with. There was likely to be a larger gap between the second and third child, while the fourth's arrival often coincided with the eldest child starting school. The very large families that had once been the norm gradually became a thing of the past. Family planning advice given by health visitors and the staff at the baby clinics did much to reduce the almost annual additions to some families. In the main, contributors had a maximum of four children, rarely five, and only one mother, a Roman Catholic, had eight children.

Most new mothers in the 1950s have admitted that their sex education both at home and in school was either negligible or at best very sketchy. Those who grew up in homes where they were the eldest girl would have had some experience of the birth process even if it was limited to the knowledge that her mother went to bed and the midwife arrived on her bicycle carrying the black bag, it was rumoured, containing the new baby, which was then left with the mother to look after. Did no child ever question how the poor infant managed to breathe in that firmly closed black bag? Or perhaps, more importantly, why it was, when the child had specifically requested a baby brother, nurse left a girl and refused to take it back and change it? Obviously we women who were of childbearing age in the 1950s were indeed naïve, because we had as small children accepted what we were told.

Most new mothers in the 1950s have admitted that their sex education both at home and in school was either negligible or at best very sketchy.

One contributor had at about the age of 4 or 5 as she rooted through an old biscuit tin containing family photographs, picture postcards and letters, found three carefully preserved pre-war wrappers from Stork margarine. Intrigued, she asked her mother for an explanation. The reply made perfect sense at the time: not only had the stork left her three babies over the years, of which she was the youngest, but a packet of margarine came with each of them. The child in question accepted this until some time later when she was told the gypsies had left her on the doorstep, thus instilling a fear of those ladies who occasionally came to the house

There was the story of the little girl who believed that mothers actually ate their babies before birth!

selling lucky heather and yards of hand-made lace, in case they had come to claim her back. Fortunately she was not gullible enough to swallow the one about the gooseberry bush. When she went to her grandfather's farm on holiday she carried out a thorough inspection of all the fruit bushes and found, if you will forgive the pun, that her search was fruitless!

So how did the 1950s mother break the news to their first offspring that they were soon to have company? This question was directed to *Mother* magazine in 1951. The letter writer was expecting her baby in three months time, and wondered how to break the news to her 5-year-old. Should it be the truth or the old story of the gooseberry bush? Women might still be naïve or ignorant, but not so the nurse giving the advice without hesitation came the very modern, sensible reply that the child must be told the truth: 'Tell him quite naturally that you are going to give him and his daddy a baby. He is sure to ask where it is now, which gives you the opportunity to tell him that it is safe and warm inside your tummy where it will stay until big enough to come out and sleep in a cot.' The advice continues

Baby sister has taken over the pram.

that the letter writer should then show the boy the cot
and baby clothes and tell him that it was going to be
such fun for them all but mother would be lost without
him being there to help her. That way,
apparently, the child would
not feel upset or jealous
when the baby arrived.
It is possible that the
actual wording the nurse
used might leave the
child with some concerns.

*A child old enough to
understand that grown ups bought
new things to replace old ones could
feel very insecure.*

There was also the story of the
little girl who believed that mothers actually ate their babies before birth! As for mummy giving
her and daddy the present of a baby, there must have
been many children who could think of presents they
would much rather have. The wise mother would take
note of any suggestions her little one might make on
that subject and have something tucked away ready to
be given as a present from the new baby.

Providing all had gone well with the first birth, the
second was more likely to take place at home. In the
late 1950s Mollie opted for this:

> Rodney was born at home during the evening, so I
> suppose Anthony [who was 20 months old] was in
> bed and slept through it all. The baby was delivered
> by a trainee midwife who told me afterwards,
> that he was the first baby she had delivered
> without supervision. The midwife appeared very
> soon afterwards! Since all our young neighbours
> were having babies too and most of them had
> their mothers come to help or to look after a
> toddler I thought I should do the same. It was a
> bad mistake. My friends were not allowed to visit

(I was supposedly sleeping) and Mum did too much
keeping the toddler 'in order'.

Two things stand out from this account; the first is the
reference to the trainee midwife. From reports that
related a similar story, we can only conclude that large
numbers of nurses took midwifery training at that time
and were working in the community. Mrs W, who had
had the rather dramatic birth involving a midwife and
two doctors in 1950, also had another home birth in
1956: 'Midwife only attended Susan's birth with trainee
nurse to see her first baby being born. Doctor called
afterwards to check on baby and mother.' Mollie in her
account highlighted the clash of ideas between mother
and daughter, her mother harking back to the days
when both mother and baby were to be kept as quiet as
possible and away from visitors. She also believed she
was doing 'the right thing' in bringing discipline into
the life of her not quite 2-year-old grandson.

On the whole the advice books of the period did not
go into the subject of what to do when the next baby
came. It was as if there was an unspoken attitude of,
'well you've had one child – made all your mistakes –
now get on with the rest of them'. And if you had the
second one very soon after the first, then the chances
were that it did indeed seem much easier that time.
Mollie's Anthony at 20 months, for example, was such
an interesting little boy that she enjoyed spending time
with him looking at books and teaching him nursery
rhymes. Fortunately the new baby seemed very easy
and happily fitted into his daily routine, so much so that
she confesses now, as do many other mothers, that they
remember little of the second baby's very early days.

How the first child reacted to the newcomer varied
greatly. Where the gap between them was slight, the

first child seemed to take little interest in the second. Jealousy was more likely to occur where the elder child had had its mother's undivided attention for several years. Suddenly he was no longer the centre of his little world and the baby's arrival could, as grandmothers were keen to point out, 'put the child's nose out of joint.'. Grandmothers who had followed the dictum that a child should not be spoilt often felt that the 1950s mothers gave their children both more attention and – disastrously – much more praise than was good for them, so it was no wonder that the little darling was now playing up. These were the grandmothers who were horrified that the child had been told the blunt truth of the forthcoming baby's whereabouts and would insist on saying things like, 'the stork is coming to your house soon', or worse, 'your mummy is going to buy another baby'. This might cause the child to wonder what it had done wrong that the parents were going to get a new one. A child old enough to understand that grown ups bought new things to replace old ones could feel very insecure. No doubt the grandmother's remarks were well intentioned but it did not help matters if they told the child that their mother would be very busy and have little time for them. Neither was it a good idea to overplay the 'Mummy's little helper' role. Even very young children could become anxious that they were not doing enough to help look after the new baby and occasionally this could lead to accidents such as the older child trying

Once a child was walking confidently, it was usually a problem to keep them in either the pram or pushchair as they were so keen to walk independently.

to dose the baby with gripe water or even the laxative Californian Syrup of Figs. Having watched mother dust the baby with talcum powder after its bath, one 'little helper' decided she had forgotten to do its head and liberally remedied the oversight, and having had some antiseptic cream rubbed on her knees and hands following a fall, big sister decided to apply the same to the baby. Poor Miss Liddiard would have been beside herself that mother should leave such items within reach of the older child, but then mother had often asked her 'little helper' to hand her items from the baby's bathtime basket.

Jealousy of the new baby could manifest itself in many ways, from surreptitiously nipping the baby's face when no one was looking to the more vicious attempt to drag it from its cot or smother it in an effort to be rid of it. The older child could also resort to tantrums or revert to early childhood behaviour such as refusing to feed himself or deliberately soiling himself. The seriously anxious child might start bedwetting or sleepwalking. All in all, it took a very patient and understanding mother to deal gently but firmly with the problems that might arise. It was here that father had a significant role to play. If he had always taken his turn in playing with or reading to his son or daughter, and had established a strong relationship with the child, then daddy could now ease some of the pressure on the mother. In some cases, fathers found it easier to bond with their second child, and by spending time with the baby, this gave the older one a chance to have his mother's attention all to himself even it was limited to that special bedtime story. Unfortunately, however much she tried to reassure her elder child that she loved him just as much as she always had, there were small children who could not understand why their parents

Brother and sister out for a walk with grandma.

needed another one. The story that this baby would be a playmate for them just did not make sense, as all it did was eat, sleep and cry! Perhaps after all, those who had their babies close together had got it right.

So the older child was now the big boy or girl. Along with so many other changes, the child was ousted from his pram and when they went out shopping, he had to sit at the handle end. Sensible mothers purchased a proper clip-on seat for the end of the pram that prevented the older one from kicking (accidentally) the baby. The Derek Pram Seat cost 27s 0d to 33s 9d. Modelled closely on the basic pushchair, its sturdy chrome framework and footrest clipped on to the end of the pram and the child was strapped in facing his mother. When the older child wanted to walk, it was easy for him to be unhooked from his straps and, once his reins were on, he could happily walk beside the pram. Once a child was walking confidently, it was usually a problem to keep them in either the pram or pushchair as they were so keen to walk independently. Unlike today when elderly ladies hold their breath when they see a tiny tot running freely along a crowded pavement ahead of its mother, the 1950s toddlers were given just so much freedom as could be achieved at the end of a pair of reins. A reluctant user of these could often be encouraged by playing horses!

The 1950s mother did not have access to the facilities that exist nowadays.

Apart from the new baby, this was often the time for someone else to appear on the scene. Parents only became aware of this addition when they heard the older child apparently talking to himself. At first they might think the conversation was with teddy, dolly or whichever soft toy was the favourite. It was when the child started talking to a vacant chair or placing his mug of juice in the place next to him at the table that the parents realised their child had an invisible or imaginary friend. Most children seemed to have them and if questioned closely they would be able to come up with quite elaborate biographies for them. Interestingly they seemed not to be concerned about the gender of their friend. Mrs J's son had a friend called Judy Max. It was assumed she was a little girl but she/he varied according to what particular exploit she was engaged in. Judy was very brave – she went off down the road to the shop on the corner all by herself – something the boy obviously dreamed of doing one day. But she could also be very naughty. It was she who picked the heads off the flowers and pulled mummy's knitting off the needles. The invisible friend became the child's alter ego, helping him to explore the boundaries of right and wrong. On the other hand, little RH had not one but two imaginary friends. These were, as far as his parents could discover, quite grown up and they both rode motorcycles, which in the 1950s was somewhat unusual for the young ladies they were reputed to be. If parents joined in the game, with mother, for example, politely offering the invisible one a biscuit or cake, it seems that the child would be more likely to grow out of the phase.

One thing that would help was to provide the child with the companionship of children of a similar age. The 1950s mother did not have access to the facilities that exist nowadays. Although crèches had been available during and just after the war, enabling women to leave their children in care while they worked in factories or other jobs vacated by men who had been called up, once demobilisation had taken place and women were no longer required to work, many of the government-sponsored day nurseries were closed. In London and other large towns some survived for the benefit of mothers who needed to work to support their families. Although they were subsidised, a weekly contribution had to be made by the mother. In London these nurseries took quite young babies as well as infants up to school age. They were very useful training grounds for young women who hoped to become nursery nurses in hospital, as well as those who were studying to become nannies in private houses. Despite the war having been a leveller of the class system, once it was over there were once again those of sufficient income and social standing to demand live-in, trained nannies to care for their children. The older generation of nannies who had often been passed down through generations of the same family were being pensioned off and replaced by younger models. These were well-educated middle-class girls who could happily take their place in the households of ducal families, high-powered, self-made business tycoons, show business personalities and members of foreign embassies, as well as the more normal upper middle-class families. For these aspiring nannies it was often a salutary experience to do their 'work experience' in a council run nursery in London's East End, such as the Elizabeth Lansbury in Poplar.

Some of the children needed bathing when they arrived at the nursery and frequently the older infants had both body and head lice.

The children they were looking after often came from some of the poorest homes; some were malnourished, so there was great emphasis on making sure that they all had plenty of milk to drink, as well as orange juice and a daily dose of cod liver oil and malt if it was needed. Babies were fed as required and a nutritious midday meal was provided for the older children, and other meals when necessary, depending on the length of time the child was in the nursery. Some of the children needed bathing when they arrived at the nursery and frequently the older infants had both body and head lice. Such things we have heard about but something that may surprise modern readers is that many of these children suffered severely from sleep deprivation.

The popular toy pedal car.

So, after the midday meal every child was put down to rest on a comfy mat on the floor. Invariably they fell asleep, some for longer than others. One trainee nanny from that period recalled that amidst all the poverty she witnessed, there was one little girl who arrived every day wearing the same dress. But that dress had obviously been washed overnight and carefully ironed, as had the little ragged ribbon that the child wore in her hair. The memory of the loving care shown by that child's mother left a lasting impression.

Day nurseries were, however, not available generally to the average 1950s mother nor, as yet, was the informal playgroup. It was towards the end of the 1950s that mothers, particularly those who lived on housing estates on the edge of towns or in country villages, got together to start a meeting place for young children. It usually needed one lively mother to suggest to two or three others that they might meet in the village or church hall one morning or afternoon a week so that their children could play together while they had a chat. The idea took off in the 1960s and by the 1970s had formed itself into a properly organised and formally recognised movement. But during most of the 1950s, children's social activities took place either in their own homes or those of neighbours and their mother's friends. In good weather the garden would be the playground it provided space to run about, play chase or simply have a bit of a rough and tumble; a simple sand pit was ideal for learning how to fill up seaside buckets or empty cartons to make sand castles, or just tip it all out or into another container. Of course there would be tears and tantrums; little Johnny had to learn not to throw sand into his friends' faces, while little Jenny had to be taught that she must not pull her playmate's hair or bite her when she wanted to push the dolls' pram.

Toys were not as plentiful then as now and many, like the essential equipment needed for babies, were handed down from older cousins or purchased second hand. This applied especially to larger items such as dolls' prams, tricycles, pedal cars and rocking horses. It was only children of the more affluent families who were likely to have the traditional style rocking horse, but the toys marketed under the Mobo logo were available to the mass market. The Bronco ride-on not only looked realistic but, by sitting on its back and pressing down on the stirrups, the horse could actually move forward. The smaller rocker was set on springs that allowed the child not only to rock backwards and forwards but also to bounce up and down. The smaller moulded plastic version was suitable for quite tiny children. Then there was the push-along horse, which could carry a small child or teddy on its back. Another firm created a simple wooden horse – really

Rocking horses were much in demand.

just a carved horse's head with a body formed from two separate pieces of padded wood that moved backwards and forwards. Unsophisticated these toys might be, but to children with imagination they could be the real thing. The well-known and much-loved tray of coloured bricks set on wheels with a handle to push it along, which was often baby's first large toy, served first as a walking aid and then became a teaching one, for colours and designs – a great source of delight as mummy or daddy joined him on the floor to help put brick upon brick and then knock the whole thing over! Later it became whatever the child imagined it was, for the child's imagination was developing all the time, from its first Christmas when, as all parents agreed, he was just as happy with the wrapping paper and cardboard boxes. There were many things that a cardboard box could be in a game of make-believe.

Most small children of the 1950s became acquainted with their local park or recreation ground. Here there was space to run about and shout without disturbing other people; if it was a park that had grassy slopes then mother might let her children climb to the top and then roly-poly down, again and again, tiring themselves out. If it was a winter that brought a good fall of snow then it would be here on these same slopes that the child would have its first taste of sledging, often

Time to get the toboggan out.

on an old tin tray rather than a piece of properly constructed equipment. While the children played under
her watchful eye, mother had a chance to sit down and
perhaps talk to other mothers.

There was always a very steep slide, its metal insert polished by hundreds of thousands of bottoms.

When the child was tired of
activity it was time for a
gentle walk homeward
through the park, per-
haps stopping to feed
the ducks on the pond,
which was carefully fenced
to make sure no one fell in.
Not so was the boating lake – not a lake with rowing
boats or punts for hire, but the shallow pool on which
many little boys learned to sail their toy boats which
usually only sailed in the bath, while bigger boys of
all ages often sailed fully rigged yachts or steamboats
on Saturday and Sunday afternoons. Municipal parks
played a huge part in the Sunday afternoons of 1950s
families. In those days, when practically everything
else was closed, they provided wide open spaces to
walk and play in as well as carefully tended gardens
to look at. Often there were football pitches and tennis
courts as well, and in many parks, in that bandstand
that had been there forever so it seemed, the local
silver or brass band might be giving a concert. Quite
apart from the health-giving benefits and the family
togetherness, the great thing was that all this was free
and available to everyone.

The park may have had a separate playground area
too, which one would certainly have found in the recreation ground provided, like the park, by the local
council. In the 1950s most of the play equipment
there had been in place for many years. It was pretty
universal throughout the country: heavy iron frames

supporting dark-green-painted woodwork, much of which was in need of repair or repainting and always seemed in need of a good application of oil to ease the creaking joints. Here the toddler was introduced to the world of older children at play. At the end of the row of three or four swings there would be one or two which were intended for small children. Instead of just a wooden seat, these swings had metal bars that formed a frame, which encased the little one on the seat. A young child loved being pushed gently back and forth, but it was a tedious and back-breaking business for the adult, especially when there were cries of 'more', which within a few weeks became 'higher'! It is amazing that there were not more serious accidents in these play areas. For a start all the equipment was firmly embedded into concrete paving slabs that covered the ground around them. The anxious mother would need to teach her child that he needed to be alert, and not to walk too close to the swings occupied by older children, who swinging back could hit the innocent bystander in the chest, or swinging forward might knock him over with their feet. There was always a very steep slide, its metal insert polished by hundreds of thousands of bottoms, as well as a turntable-type thing that you had to hold on to the outer edge of one of the horizontal bars that radiated from the centre and then, giving it a push, run round until it started to turn, at which point you jumped on and sat down. The danger was getting a foot caught and being dragged round. Equally lethal were the battering ram-type swing that held any number of children at once and the wigwam-shaped object that not only rotated but went in towards the centre and out again. The reader has probably detected a certain loathing for this kind of playground equipment. Certainly the modern wooden structures, which demand ingenuity for climbing and ropes for swinging, all set in sand or upon special safety surfaces, are much preferred. These days, grandmother can enjoy her visits to the park far more than she ever did either as a child or a mother!

Apart from finding companions to play with in the park or recreation ground, there were two other places where the under 5s were able to socialise with other children. Certainly in the early 1950s most churches still held Sunday School in the early afternoon, and accepted little ones from 3 onwards. Here they got to sing choruses or recite little verses with actions, or draw pictures. A very simple story and a going home prayer would complete the hour they spent there. This time brought them not only into contact with other children but also offered them the chance to join the summer outing – a picnic perhaps and games in a large garden somewhere or a trip by coach to the seaside. Although one or other of their parents might come too, the experience was good preparation for the day when they would eventually start school. During the second half of the 1950s many churches held Sunday School at the same time as the morning service; the children attended that with their parents but were taken off to another hall or room for their own activities just before the sermon began. Sermons tended to be much longer in those days!

Children over 3, and little girls in particular, might be enrolled in a weekly dance class.

Children over 3 and little girls in particular, might be enrolled in a weekly dance class. This enhanced most children's natural ability to move to music; it also gave little girls the chance to dress up and 'show off' while at

Riding the grocery delivery man's horse was better
than her rocking horse. This was a popular pastime for
children in the 1950s. What would health and safety make
of that today?

the same time they learned discipline from the teacher.
The very young quickly imitated the older ones and
amazed their mothers with their prowess when it came
to the end of term concert. Boys too could join but
there seemed to be reluctance on the part of some parents to consider a dancing class as quite the right place
for their sons. Dancing classes run by private dancing
schools and academies cost money, the termly fees
of which might well be beyond the means of many.
However, for those who lived in a large town, it was

possible that the local Co-operative Society ran, among its educational groups, weekly dance and drama classes for the Co-op Juniors. For a small weekly fee of a few pence, a child could start what might become a lifetime interest. But that's another story.

8

The Premature Baby

Huge advances have been made in so many different spheres of medical science since the 1950s and probably none more so than in the care given to premature babies. Most of us have read, or may even have first-hand knowledge of babies that have been born as early as twenty-six weeks – and have survived. We may have seen television pictures of these tiny scraps of humanity whose weight is calculated in ounces rather than pounds and whose measurements make the average adult hand seem overly large. Thanks to the special neonatal baby care units in our larger hospitals, modern machines that mimic the womb, and the right medication and treatment, combined with the skill and compassionate care of the medical and nursing teams, most of these babies eventually achieve what would have been their normal birth weight and the majority of them catch up unscathed with full-term babies.

This is what happened to Mrs S. Within the last decade, Mrs S's first baby, which turned out to be twins, decided to make their entry into this world fifteen weeks before they should have done, that is at two days short of twenty-five weeks. At birth the two little boys were given a fifty-fifty chance of survival and sadly one died within a few hours. Little R, however, although he weighed only 750g hung on to life assisted by the most up-to-date machinery and dedicated nursing care available in the special baby care unit of his local hospital. There he remained for the next fifteen weeks. During that time his parents were constantly in attendance and fortunately Mrs S had a plentiful supply of breast milk, which she was able to express to help feed R and which was said to have assisted greatly in his recovery. Against all the odds, the little boy flourished and on what would have been the due date for his birth, having reached a weight of 5½lb, the proud parents took him home.

In comparison with stories like this, it comes as a shock to read in the various manuals in use in the 1950s that the definition of a premature baby was one that may have arrived early but also one that was below 5½lb in weight. *The Mothercraft Manual*, which in its usual austere way makes us so aware of the changes that have taken place in the use of language in the last sixty years, tells us that we should remember:

> These infants are feeble in every way, their organs not being ready to carry on the functions of maintaining heat, breathing, digesting, etc. The whole aim must be to plan everything so that they are handled as little as possible, kept warm by external heat and given the easiest food, as their digestive organs will be upset. The first thing is to prevent their ever getting

cold; once cold or chilled all chance of maintaining their feeble little lives has probably gone.

One wonders what Miss Liddiard would have made of those babies born nowadays weighing less than a 2lb bag of sugar. If, as is likely, the baby was born at home and was, by the standards of the day, far too early in its development, she might have advocated what one midwife did, wrap the child in a shawl, place it close to the fire in the hearth and turn her attention to the mother. By the time the mother had been settled, the baby would have given up any fight for life.

The Nestlé handbook also contained a short chapter on premature births, noting that the number of these had decreased greatly in recent years mainly due to the antenatal care that was available to all expectant mothers from their local health centres, which ensured that they received the correct medical care and advice on food and essential vitamins required for their general well-being. Readers were warned that it was possible for premature confinements to become a habit, probably because something was lacking in their diet, so it was important that anyone who had given birth prematurely inform their health carers as early as possible in their next pregnancy.

Those babies that were very early and thus severely underweight and underdeveloped would have been taken into hospital, placed in an incubator and given specialist nursing. However, not every hospital had these facilities so mother and baby could be taken to one that had, but this was often many miles from the patient's home. That could present problems for the family if there were other small children to be cared for. But since the numbers of births requiring intensive hospital care was very small in comparison to similar ones today, the books did not concentrate on them. Instead, both the Nestlé book and *The Mothercraft Manual* gave detailed advice as to the procedure necessary in the event of the early birth, say at seven months,

All dusters and floor-cleaning cloths were to be rinsed in an antiseptic solution.

taking place at home, or if it had been in a hospital allowing the mother and baby to go home to be looked after. We are told that although it would be preferable for the baby to be cared for in a separate room where a constant temperature and humidity could be maintained, it was realised that this was not always possible. Whichever room the baby was to be kept in had to be stripped down to bare essentials, all unnecessary furniture, carpets and curtains removed and everything else made spotlessly clean. All dusters and floor-cleaning cloths were to be rinsed in an antiseptic solution. The room should be heated, preferably with a coal fire, and kept at an even temperature of about 70°F (21°C). Today's reader may question why the recommended heating was by a coal fire, especially at a time before the introduction of smokeless fuel. The answer is twofold: first, coal was the most common form of domestic heating in the 1950s and, second, the chimney maintained a good circulation of air. Where necessary a room thermometer would be provided along with any other necessary equipment.

More interesting than the formal advice books was the account in *Mother* magazine by the reader whose second daughter was declared to be premature when she was born in 1958. During one of her last antenatal checks the doctor had said that she thought the baby was rather small. As nothing more was said on the subject the mother, let us call her Mrs X as she was not identified in the article, carried on as usual until she was confined at home and delivered a little girl who was indeed small, weighing in at just 4lb 10oz, considerably below

No visitors were allowed in the room and the fire was kept burning day and night.

the 7 – 7½lb of the average baby of the time. As was usual after a midwife delivery, the doctor made a routine visit and it was then that Mrs X was told that her baby was regarded as premature, that is not fully developed, so would require the special nursing care of the 'Prem. Nurse'. Apparently at that time in her county, and probably many others throughout the land, there existed a home nursing service for premature babies. There was just one nurse for the whole county who travelled by car between those who needed her, bringing with her all the necessary equipment required. This service not only helped the overworked hospital units but also relieved mothers of stress by making them feel happier to be in their home environment and thus making the baby more content because of its contact with its mother. Had she needed it, Mrs X would have been provided with the special cot for nursing premature babies, but the one she had was considered suitable and was warmed with hot-water bottles prior to the baby being put in it. Nurse, gowned and masked, weighed the little girl then sponged her with olive oil. Mrs X wrote:

I learned that she must not be bathed for a while, as the shock of coming into the world is enough for the tiny body to absorb to begin with. Neither was she to receive food for forty-eight hours.

Mother was then instructed on how to keep the cot at an even temperature by changing the hot-water bottles every hour and how to place the blankets over the baby to ensure warmth without their weighing too heavily upon her. The nurse then departed:

No sooner had she gone than the baby started to cry. This went on all night and she only stopped at 7 am from exhaustion. There was certainly no question of her not getting sufficient oxygen through failing to use her lungs!

Every mother reading that must feel intense sympathy for poor Mrs X. Unfortunately we are not told at what time the nurse had left so we have no idea of quite how long it was the poor baby cried. But how did the mother manage to get through the night denying the instinctive reaction to pick up the baby and comfort it? And what relief she must have felt when nurse arrived at eleven o'clock. After the wash in olive oil nurse gave baby some glucose water from a spoon, which seemed to satisfy her hunger a little, but it was decided that mother could start feeding her that afternoon. Nurse had brought with her a sterile container that held four tiny 1oz bottles, eight 2oz bottles and a teat. A ¼oz of milk mixture was put into each of the larger bottles and with the added water it looked, according to Mrs X, more like blue-coloured water than milk. This was the start of a three-hourly feeding schedule. Glucose water was put into the smaller bottles for the baby should she wake before her feeding time or if she still seemed hungry after the feed. The prem. nurse came to visit twice daily: at eleven o'clock for the olive oil bath and again at four o'clock in the afternoon to prepare the bottles and monitor how the feeding was going. The hot-water bottles were reheated while mother fed and changed the baby. This was the only time mother was allowed to handle her daughter. No visitors were allowed in the room and the fire was kept burning day and night. There were some problems of course: the baby developed a rash on her bottom and from the fact that she soiled every nappy it was decided that sugar should be cut out of her feeds. However, by the tenth day the baby's weight had reached 5½lb – that magic figure – and for the first time Mrs X was able to bath her daughter in soap and water. From that same day the baby stopped waking for a night feed and before the two weeks were up, nurse had decided she had done her work and was no longer needed. Mrs X had written her account to give thanks for the effective and thorough care she and her daughter, by then a lively and sturdy 3-year-old, had received and to reassure other mothers of premature babies.

One cannot help marvelling that such home care was freely available to those who needed it under the National Health Service in the 1950s. And what is also interesting is that much of the practice described by Mrs X in her account was in fact a précis of the material in the nursing handbooks, so we know how the prem. nurses were being trained at that time. What stalwart women they must have been, sometimes driving long distances between patients, ready day and night for any emergency. Perhaps their work might provide an interesting TV sequel to *Call the Midwife*!

9

Adoption

*I*n the days before infertility treatment was available, the only course open to the childless couple who longed for a baby was to adopt someone else's child. Throughout history it had been accepted that for whatever reason, some children were brought up in families that were not theirs by birth. It was common practice for those who could afford it to take on the responsibility for the upbringing of one or more children of a less fortunate relation or close friend. Often these arrangements were of an informal nature, the child in question being fully aware of his or her original parentage. On the other hand, many wealthy men and women who had no direct heirs adopted children who were brought up as their own kin and in the knowledge that one day they would inherit vast estates. Sometimes people actually adopted their own children – the man who had fathered children by his mistress, or a woman who had secretly given birth to a child out of wedlock but was later able to pretend the child had been born to someone else.

The social stigma attached to unmarried girls and women becoming pregnant was very strong in the 1950s, possibly much more than it had been in the nineteenth century. In late Victorian times, an indiscretion amongst the middle and upper classes could be hushed up by sending the offender to live either in the country or even abroad where the resulting child could be fostered, perhaps for good. If the girl was accepted back into the family in time, having 'completed her studies or travels abroad', then it was possible that when the child reached adulthood or a suitable age then it might be introduced into the family as a distant relation. In poorer families 'a chance baby', as they were known in Suffolk for example, born to an older sister, was absorbed into the already large family and frequently grew up unaware that the woman known as mother was really grandmother. If the pregnant girl was rejected by her family then she had to resort to the workhouse to have the baby and if she was unable to earn a living sufficient to support both her and the child, then the child probably ended up either being sent to a children's home or an orphanage, or remaining in the workhouse until of an age to start work.

By the 1950s the horrors of being thrown into the workhouse had ceased to be a threat but the moral attitude prevailing at the time meant that the girl who discovered she was pregnant had to face what was probably a worse

Throughout the country there were mother and baby homes of various sizes to which the unmarried woman could be referred by her doctor or minister of religion.

ordeal: of telling her parents. The fear of the wrath of
outraged parents led some young girls to attempt to hide
their condition, some of them even going through labour
on their own and then leaving the baby in some place
where they hoped it would be found and taken care of.
Others realised that they needed parental support and so
confronted them head on. The reaction of many parents
was one of deep shame. They felt that they had been
let down by their daughter but at the same time they
blamed themselves for not forcing stronger moral principles upon her. In the midst of all the recriminations,
at some point someone, usually the mother, would utter
those immortal words,: 'whatever will people think?' It
was still true that while a young man could sow his wild
oats, girls were expected to come to their wedding nights
as virgins. What no one seemed
to have realised was that
this might have held true
at a time when the bride
was barely 14 and only
just entering puberty
but times had changed
in the last 400 or so years.

*Those who could not knit
or sew were encouraged to do so and
they were expected to help with the
domestic work within the house.*

Unfortunately attitudes had not and, respectability being
the watchword of the 1950s, it was the girl who bore
the brunt of recriminations for her condition. She found
herself labelled as a 'brazen hussy' and various other
hurtful titles. Few had any sympathy with her plight,
even those among her close friends who might well have
found themselves in a similar condition. Depending on
her age, the first concern of her parents was whether
she could she be married to the father of the child. If the
baby was the result of a relationship between a young
couple who had been together for some time, then what
became known as 'shot-gun wedding' was likely to

take place, followed in due time by the birth of a 'premature' baby. 'People', that is friends and neighbours, were well aware of the facts, but respectability had been preserved.

It was a different story for those girls who were either too young to be married off or those where the father of the child refused to accept any responsibility. The girl's parents were then faced with a decision: did they aid their daughter by offering her support throughout her pregnancy and help her bring up the child in the future, or did they try to pretend that nothing had happened until just before the birth and then send her away to have the child and insist that it be placed immediately for adoption. There were so many things to be considered – not only what the neighbours would say – such as what effect the baby would have on other members of the family, the financial resources of the parents, the girl's own future chances for pursuing a career or making 'a good marriage' later and so on. With hindsight, given the information that is now available to us, it is difficult to review dispassionately either the dilemma faced by the parents or the vulnerable young women, who were told that mothering a baby when young and unmarried was weak and selfish but that giving up the child for adoption showed true love, bravery and unselfishness.

Although by the 1950s the State had started to take control of much of our lives, the care of unwanted children was mainly in the hands of voluntary philanthropic or religious groups. Throughout the country there were mother and baby homes of various sizes to which the unmarried woman could be referred by her doctor or minister of religion. These hostels could be in lovely old country houses set in parkland, or

gaunt-looking town houses in the heart of an industrial town. Some were large and frightening, others
small and friendly; it all depended who was responsible for running them. Much has been written and
screened about the Magdalen houses in Ireland, run by
Catholic nuns who obtained financial support for them
by operating laundries in which the 'fallen women', as
the unmarried mothers were known, worked. Many
of these women seem to have been condemned there
for life. However, in England, the length of stay in a
home or shel-
ter was about
three months,
six weeks before the
expected birth date and
six weeks after it. Here, the
Anglican Sisters, Salvationists
or whichever group it was
that ran the home would try to
teach the women not only the error
of their ways, but how to prepare for
their child just in case they were able to keep it. Those
who could not knit or sew were encouraged to do so
and they were expected to help with the domestic
work within the house. Those who needed any special medical treatment received it and those in charge
made sure that all the women were properly fed and
drank all their milk. Although the homes relied in the
main on support from charitable sources, one assumes
that those inmates whose parents could afford it
were expected to make a contribution towards their
daughter's maintenance.

After the baby was born, for the next six weeks the
women did everything for him that any new mother
would. During this difficult period, while bonding

These babies stayed in hospital until they were cleared medically for release and were then handed over to a foster mother for six weeks before being placed with adoptive parents.

with the infant, they were given the opportunity to decide if they really wished to go ahead with the adoption of their child. Often the girl had no choice in the matter, it was decided for her. If that was to be the case they were encouraged to knit or sew garments for their baby, or make or purchase a toy that it could take with it when it went to its new parents. Finally the day came for the irrevocable break. Once the baby had gone she would have no knowledge of his whereabouts or ever be able to contact him. To ensure that this was upheld, once the child was officially adopted, he would be granted a shortened birth certificate bearing the name his adoptive parents had given him, in place of the one on the certificate issued when the birth was initially registered which contained the name the mother had chosen for her baby, as well as all the relevant details of parentage. The mother was then free to return, childless, to either her previous life or start a new one.

The couple wishing to adopt would probably approach the agency that ran the mother and baby home and, having been interviewed, provided the necessary references and been accepted, they would be informed when a suitable baby might be available. Once the mother had left the home, the prospective parents would then visit and decide if the child was for them. From this we have the romantic notion that was often fed to adopted children, that their adoptive parents had been shown a whole room full of babies and they had chosen this one from all the rest.

Not all unmarried mothers had their babies in these homes. Many carried on in their own home until the birth of the child in the local maternity hospital. In this case they were either spared or denied, depending on your point of view, the opportunity to bond with their baby for more than the eight or ten days of the normal confinement. If they were placing their child for adoption they and their parents would have discussed the options. In some cases, the child was taken away from them immediately after the birth; there are reports that some girls were not even told the sex of their child. These babies stayed in hospital until they were cleared medically for release and were then handed over to a foster mother for six weeks before being placed with adoptive parents. Many of the others stayed their time and then, carrying their baby, they left with their mother or both parents and were driven in a taxi to an office where they handed over the baby to a complete stranger. One woman reported that having done this her parents never ever referred to the episode again.

It is easy to over sentimentalise what to us may seem a harsh system, the worst aspect of which may have been the splitting up of twins although even that is understandable to some extent. Normal families would have been able to get used to the idea of having two babies at once and could perhaps even get some practice in, but given the shortness of time that adoptive parents had before they collected their baby, one can understand that the idea of twins might be daunting, quite apart from the additional expense that would involve.

So far we have only looked at the young unmarried woman who was forced to give up her child, something she may have bitterly regretted all her life. But what of the older woman, who may well have been married, who actively sought adoption for her child? This is the woman who did not attempt to rid herself of a child with an illegal abortion which might have proved an easier, if more dangerous, option. Instead she went through the pregnancy and birth, determined to give her child the best start in life by giving it up for adoption.

This is as much of Lilian's story that is relevant to us. Born in London in 1926, she had married, probably just after the war, when she was about 20. In 1948 she was admitted to the Royal Free Hospital where, sadly, she suffered severe complications following the stillbirth of her first child. The advice she and her husband were given then was that it would be dangerous for her ever to attempt another pregnancy. How much that affected their later relationship is not known but in 1956 Lilian was granted a divorce on the grounds of her husband's adultery. By that time she was holding down a responsible job and earning a good salary as a telephonist in a large London company. Amongst those who worked there was a man in his mid- forties who was employed as a delivery driver. The nature of his work was such that he came and went at intervals, sometimes of several weeks at a time. The sort of friendship that often occurs in the workplace grew up between them, he being easy-going and relaxed with a good sense of humour. Lilian, who was in the throes of her divorce, found him easy to talk to and very understanding. She knew, of course, that Derek was married but his wife had moved out of London and it appeared they rarely saw each other. It was not long before the friendship deepened and at the end of 1957 Lilian discovered she was pregnant.

> *'There was one toilet between twelve people and no bathroom for general use.'*

One can imagine the mental turmoil this must have caused her, bearing in mind her previous medical history, but the upshot was that she and Derek decided to set up home together. From the start it was a stormy relationship but they both tried to make a go of it for the sake of the baby, a beautiful little boy who was born in April 1958 at the Royal Free Hospital. Although Derek was thrilled with his new son, he made no attempt to seek a legal separation from his wife, deep down, Lilian became convinced that when he was away on the company's business he visited his wife. When the baby was 6 months old they were given notice to quit by their landlord. The accommodation they found in Kentish Town was probably typical of much in London at that time when large early nineteenth-century three- or four-storey houses were divided up into one- and two-room living areas. In a letter a few months later Lilian wrote: 'It was a dreadful house, dirty and dilapidated but rooms were unfurnished and the landlord accepted the baby. There was one toilet between twelve people and no bathroom for general use.' The rent charged was £2 5s a week, with electricity having to be paid for via a slot meter housed outside the rooms, which left them vulnerable to being rifled – indeed they were on several occasions, leaving her having to find the money to replace that which was taken. But from Lilian's point of view, 'just about the worst thing that could have happened' was the discovery that she was pregnant again. Her son would be barely 18 months old when the new baby arrived. By now life with Derek had become unbearable; his refusal to commit to her led to constant rows and so at her request he left. She was then forced to seek help from the National Assistance Board who granted her £3 10s a week on top of the £1 10s Derek gave her.

Her rent then rose by 5s so she was left with £2 10s for food, gas, electricity and essentials for the baby. The final blow came when her landlord, realising there was another child on the way, gave her notice to quit.

Lilian decided that the only option open to her was to have the unborn child adopted and so she set the necessary measures in motion. She sensibly realised that, on her own, she could manage to support herself and her son. She had plans to place him in a day nursery and return to work, hoping that she would earn around the £9 that would be sufficient to support them both. But another baby would make that impossible. For the third time Lilian found herself under the care of the maternity services at the Royal Free Hospital. She talked matters over with both a caseworker for the National Adoption Society and the hospital's almoner, and Lilian asked that the new baby should go straight from the hospital to foster parents until such time as he would be adopted. Payment had to be made to the foster parents and Lilian's brother had agreed to help meet this cost. When Lilian met the adoption caseworker she had her son with her, described as 'a lovely child with fair curly hair'. This was a useful indication of what the unborn child might look like. The baby, another boy, was born in September and after six weeks with a foster mother, was taken home by the couple whose dream of having a child to love and cherish finally came true. When the legalities of the adoption were finally completed Lilian wrote to the Adoption Society:

> I am pleased to hear that the adoption of David has been completed. As the months have gone by I am even more sure that I did the right thing in parting with him, as I still haven't got a place of my own to

live in. I have a fairly well paid job though, which is some consolation, but I doubt if I could bring up two children on it. I am glad he has settled down so well in his new home and I am happy he has gone to a couple who will do their best to give him the future and security he should have.

It is a pity that Lilian did not live long enough to hear for herself of the loving home life her son had had or to learn that eventually her two sons happily found each other – and the half siblings that Derek had with his wife!

By today's standards adoption procedures in the 1950s may have been very informal, appearing to lack the careful and very lengthy scrutiny of social workers. Yet the majority of children who were adopted at that time grew up in loving homes. The only real criticism one can make of the system was that most adopting couples wanted new or very young babies, which meant that toddlers and older children who were put up for adoption for one reason or another might have had to go instead to a children's home.

10

Holidays

*T*he favourite conversational standby for hair-dressers for the last fifty years has been either 'where are you going for your summer holi-day?' or 'where did you go for your holiday?' You will notice that in the second question the word summer has been dropped because nowadays people not only take holidays at any time of the year, but many take two or even three. Not so long ago it had become cus-tomary for families to have their main summer holiday somewhere in Europe where the sun was guaranteed, plus a winter break skiing in Switzerland or Austria and the October half-term holiday in the south of France. With the development of the Disney theme parks among other attractions of that ilk, families packed their flight bags and took off for California and Florida – the less adventurous or more financially straightened made do with Paris. From the growth of air travel and package tours in the late 1950s, even remote areas of the globe are accessible and tiny babies and toddlers have become seasoned travellers as their parents took to camping in France or Germany, staying in hotels in Spain, spending a month in an Italian villa or visiting relations in the Far East and Australasia.

A booming economy and longer paid holidays contributed to a scenario beyond the comprehension of most young couples in the 1950s. At that time most firms gave their employees one week's paid leave. In industrial areas in the north and the midlands, the whole factory would shut down for a week, and those who could afford it would go away during that time. The problem was that this created almost a mini invasion of the local seaside resorts like Blackpool or Morecambe for those weeks when the different factories were closed. The influx also meant that you might find that some of your neighbours were guests in the same boarding house or fellow passengers if you had opted for a coach tour to the Lake District or the Highlands of Scotland. For those in other parts of the country who were not affected by what were still known as Wakes Weeks, annual holidays were usually spread over the summer months of June to early September.

How one spent the week depended mainly on finance. Those with young children found it easier to opt for days out. For the family it was a novelty to have father at home for a whole week, so the most had to be made of it. At a time when there was little spare money in the majority of households with a young family, it was often difficult to find spare cash to put aside to finance outings. One way of doing this was to pay into a holiday club. These were informal groups usually run in connection with a local public house. Starting in the New Year, and usually on a Friday evening, the club treasurer would collect the small subscriptions of a shilling or two, which meant that by the time the holiday came round, several pounds might have accrued to the saver. After the holiday, the club members started saving again for Christmas.

The concept of the holiday-at-home had grown in popularity during the war and the years that immediately followed it. The idea was that one took advantage of whatever facilities were available in one's locality. This meant going to the local park and enjoying the freedom for the children to run around or for parents to join them in playing games or flying kites. If the weather was good, mother would pack a picnic – egg and cress or fish paste sandwiches, some home-made buns or jam tarts, all washed down with orange squash or a bottle of Corona soft drink or Tizer. The whole day could be spent in the park and the only money the parents would need to lay out might be on ice cream bought from a kiosk. If it stocked Eldorado, father might return with two wrapped slices of ice cream and four flat wafers to make a sort of sandwich for him and mother, while for the children there would be small solid rounds, encircled by thin card which was removed as the ice cream was placed in a crisp cornet.

Other options for a day out, without travelling more than perhaps a bus ride, entailed just that. If one lived in a large town, it was possible that the local bus company would provide a 'Rover' ticket that enabled families to travel to different areas of the town at a greatly reduced fare. This gave people the chance to explore what was on their doorstep as it were: other parks, river walks and woods, historic sites and so on, or quite simply to take the opportunity to visit with friends or relations. Depending on the weather, one might include a day at the local open-air swimming pool. Again this was a fairly cheap way to entertain the family as, unlike nowadays when pools operate in fairly short sessions, it was possible to spend certainly a whole morning or afternoon, if not the whole day, for one entry fee. Most good lidos had a paddling pool in which the very young could enjoy themselves, and there was also a spectators' area, so if baby was very young, then mother could sit out with it and watch, while father took the older children in the pool and tried to teach them to swim. The idea of mothers attending special classes in a heated indoor pool teaching their tiny babies to enjoy being in water and perhaps learning to swim, was still a step too far for the 1950s mother. As, indeed, in some cases, was the very idea of mother actually donning a swimming costume.

Although swimming pools provided a great deal of fun, there was no denying that it was not the same as the real thing: a day on the beach at the seaside.

Although swimming pools provided a great deal of fun, there was no denying that it was not the same as the real thing: a day on the beach at the seaside. One of the great advantages of living on an island is that much of the urban population has reasonable access to the coast and, whenever possible, we seem drawn to spend time by the sea. For some it is the lure of the large resorts which specialise in catering for the entertainment of visitors, while for those who prefer a more tranquil setting and are prepared to go off the well-trodden routes, there are quiet little fishing villages with a small beach area, or, as a complete contrast, there are the long stretches of shingle beach such as those parts of Dorset and Suffolk, from which to catch fish or paddle. Best of all was a sheltered area with miles of golden sands running gently into a calm sea where children could safely play. Possibly the only drawback to such an idyllic spot was that everyone else wanted to share it. During the 1950s most townspeople visited their nearest seaside resort, perhaps to stay for their whole week's holiday, or as day-trippers as part of their holiday-at-home, or regularly at weekends throughout the summer. They were able to do this because their local bus and train companies ran regular excursions at affordable fares. It was now that the folding pushchair was so useful. Once the family had staked a claim to a good spot, deck chairs procured for mother and father and towels spread out for the older children, then baby could be put down for his nap in the pushchair. Mother would have made sure that she had brought the sunshade that fitted on the chair; if not a large umbrella would be opened, and, with its handle firmly embedded in the sand to stop it flying away, this could be adjusted to make sure baby was kept in the shade.

Assuming that the weather was warm enough, the toddlers and slightly older children would put on their swimming costumes.

The family would have brought various bags with them: one would have all the paraphernalia the baby needed, another would hold the other children's swim-wear and spare clothes – in case of accidents – and then there would be the bag with the picnic food and drink. Assuming that the weather was warm enough, the toddlers and slightly older children would put on their swimming costumes. By the 1950s we are beginning to say goodbye to the hand-knitted one-piece garments that had still been popular beachwear in the 1940s; but of course from 1940–45, perhaps even later in some places, most of the beaches were closed to non-military personnel. Many children dispensed with designated swimwear, their mothers considering it quite in order for them simply to strip off down to their knickers or pants, while babies often discarded their nappies and crawled around naked, soaking up valuable vitamin D. Sun hats were worn if it was very hot but in the early 1950s no one knew anything about harmful ultraviolet rays and the need to use special creams or lotions to prevent damage to the skin. If a child looked as if it was going red, then a garment was put on, and if necessary a bit of Nivea or Astral cold cream applied at bed time, after a bath had removed all the sand from various crevices in the little bodies.

Mother was likely to have put on a cotton dress or skirt and blouse, covered by the inevitable cardigan - in case it turns chilly.

Mum and dad might or might not change their clothes before they got down to the business of showing their offspring how to make sand pies before progressing to the major work of building a sandcastle. Mother was likely to have put on a cotton dress or skirt and blouse, covered by the inevitable cardigan – in case it turns chilly. She might be wearing sandals, in which case she will have dispensed with her stockings, surreptitiously wriggled out of when no one was looking, rolled up and placed inside her shoes, ready to be put back on when it was going home time. Once men had taken on the responsibility of family life, they were often much more reluctant to bare their bodies. Sadly, the picture postcard caricature of the man with a

The new baby's first visit to the seaside.

knotted handkerchief on his head and his grey flannel trousers rolled up to his knees was a common sight on the beach. Casual leisure wear was still to come for the average man; when he visited the coast he wore what he would wear to go out, and that included a white shirt and tie. The photograph of the family walking along a seaside promenade with the carrycot illustrates this beautifully. Judging by the fact that the baby, Mary, was born in mid-February, this picture must have been taken by a professional promenade photographer in April or May. Possibly it was Easter or Whitsun. This picture has much to tell us about the period. From the clothes that were worn, we may perhaps deduce that it was a Sunday, as mother was wearing her tweed two-piece while father has on his best suit complete with waistcoat. This suit and his trilby hat have the hall-marks of the clothing that was issued to all demobilised troops from 1946 onwards. Father has come prepared for all weathers, hence the raincoat he carries, while

The same family on the beach a year or so later.

the two girls aged 8 and 11 are wearing the regula-
tion school summer dresses of check gingham. Both
are wearing coats, for the younger one it is her Sunday
best, while the older girl has on her school uniform
gaberdine raincoat. One has the impression that the
family will not be going to sit on the beach on this
occasion. Possibly this was the new baby's first outing
away from home.

A year or two later and the family are again shown
enjoying a day at the seaside, this time on the beach.
As the snapshot was probably taken by father, we
do not have the chance to see if he is more casually
dressed for sitting upon the
golden sands at Yarmouth,
but note that although
mother is wearing a
summer dress and is
bare legged, she is still
wearing her two-string
pearl necklace. Mary's two
sisters are wearing the fashion-
able ruched nylon bathing suits of the period while
the young Mary sports a cotton sun-suit, patterns

*For some children this first
beach pony ride might waken a
desire to learn to ride.*

for which appeared in *Mother* magazine as well as *Woman's Weekly*. It is interesting to see, too, that Mary has the hairstyle common for little girls at that time: a side parting with a section of hair that was brushed across the head being held by a ribbon tied with a bow on the opposite side to the parting. Most little girls in the 1950s wore their hair like this until they were about 7 and decided they wished to grow their hair and have plaits, or pigtails as they were more generally called.

The third of Mary's seaside photographs shows her on a family holiday taken further from home, this time in Blackpool where we see a happy 3-year-old digging into that vast area that was left when the tide went out. This could be a typical British summer holiday scene of around 1954–55. The weather was chilly as we can see from the little girl's cardigan and the coats of some of those in the background, but there are also brave souls in bathing costumes at the water's edge. Interesting is the group of figures behind Mary, a man with two children, all dressed for cold weather. The man is wearing a suit with collar and tie but he has his trousers rolled up to his knees! Was it only with the advent of foreign holidays late in the 1950s that parents adopted casual clothes and even wore swimwear on the beach? However he was dressed, fathers usually enjoyed relaxing and playing with their little ones on the beach.

Was it the development of the Victorian railway system and the introduction of excursions to the seaside for working families that brought about the great art of building sandcastles, or did that go back to long, long before, with fathers teaching their children the basics of brick making? Giving mother a chance to have a rest for a while, father could show his child how

The tide goes out such a long way in Blackpool.

to dig out the sand with the toy spade and fill the little metal, later plastic, bucket. Once the baby had got over the pour it in and then up end the bucket to pour it out again, he progressed to the stage of digging deeper to reach damp sand, which when patted well down in the bucket would, when inverted, turn out a perfectly firm shape. From that, the next move was designing a mound to form a rudimentary castle. It is doubtful that a toddler would remember years later, when it came up in a history class, that he had probably often made a motte and bailey castle on the beach!

The latest fashion in bathing suits for little girls.

There were other delights to be found on the beach, among them the Punch and Judy show which always drew a large crowd of children who laughed uproariously at Mr Punch's often vicious antics, causing concerned parents to worry about the effect such behaviour might have on their children. Much gentler, though to some perhaps a bit frightening, was a ride on a donkey or a pony along the sand. For a family of two or three

The donkey ride was a real treat.

children this could prove expensive at 1s per child, and exasperating for parents when one of them having demanded to be included in the treat, decided halfway through the ride that he didn't want to continue and had to be removed from the animal's back in tears. For some children this first beach pony ride might waken a desire to learn to ride. A magazine contributor shared an amusing anecdote. Visiting friends who had recently acquired a pony for their small daughter, she was somewhat nonplussed as she watched the little girl showing off her skill in the meadow. The pony and rider started off from the gate towards the centre of the field when suddenly the pony stopped, turned and ambled back to the gate again where it stopped. Seeing her bemused look, the new owners explained to their visitor that the pony had been retired recently from beach work but had yet to forget his previous training of when to turn to go back to base.

If it appears that we have dwelt too long discussing the seaside that is because that was how most people with small children spent their free time. Although a great number of men, and women too, who had served in the forces during and after the war had learned to drive, cars were very expensive and in short supply until the car factories were able to get back into production again. We have to recognise too that in the 1950s, in spite of the war having supposed to be a great leveller, there was still a feeling amongst large sections of the population that car ownership, much like having a telephone in the home, 'was not for the likes of us'. Thus very few ordinary people owned cars during the 1950s. In most streets in the average town, the sight of a car parked outside a house was a rarity; often it was a sign that the doctor had been called. Tradesmen usually had vans or in some cases still used horse-drawn vehicles, but salesmen who travelled long distances to show their wares and take orders needed a car. Those firms who provided a car for their salesmen made it clear that it was for business only and was not insured for carrying the family on pleasure trips.

So, apart from the wealthy who could afford a car for leisure, most of the population relied on the bicycle as a means of transport. The district nurse and the midwife came to visit on bicycles, even in country districts; the insurance man collecting his weekly or monthly premiums called on his cycle, as did the piano tuner, the sweep, the Hoover and the Singer service engineers, and many others too. Walls resurrected their pre-war iconic ice cream vending tricycles which were eventually displaced by the travelling vans selling soft ice cream. Instead of the later jangled version of *Greensleeves* to alert the children of the neighbourhood, the Walls man rang his tricycle bell. In better-off areas, householders had a card with a large blue capital W, which they placed in the front window indicating that the householder wished the ice cream man to call.

Since practically everyone rode a bicycle, many young couples who had been in the habit of going off on cycling trips at weekends or for their annual holiday, once they became parents, decided that as soon as he was old enough, baby should come too. Often a seat was either purchased or home-made and then fitted on to the back of one or other of the parents' bicycles. When there were two children, the younger was likely to be installed behind mother, the older with father. In the case of a young boy, he might have a seat fitted in front of father on the cross bar. Occasionally, one would see a small child seated in what was a variation of the old soapbox on wheels, attached to the back of the adult's cycle by what looked like the shafts of a pony cart. Those who cycled in those days and those who as children had been transported on cycles, all remark that things are very different nowadays. Mutterings about health and safety inspectors and the lack of safety headgear can be heard, along with a certain amount of amazement that no one could recall ever being involved in an accident with small children. The answer lies, of course, in the very different road conditions then. Not only were there so few cars on the road and speed was also much lower than nowadays, but there was also an absence of the juggernaut lorries that we now accept as commonplace. The pace of life really was slower then and as such families could take holidays safely using their bicycles to get them into the countryside surrounding their local town.

A step up from the bicycle and a bit closer to a car was the motorcycle. For many young men it was a dream machine, the possession of which they justified by using it for transport to and from work. They may also have found it a way of courting the more adventurous young woman who was happy to ride pillion. These couples were able to travel much further afield for their holidays, often visiting areas not accessible by regular bus or train services. Once the baby arrived on the scene, then it was a question of investing in a sidecar to attach to the bike if they wished to continue with days out away from home. On the other hand, those who were keen walkers often continued their hobby, carrying baby on father's back in a special holder. Whatever way they did it, most people tried to have a holiday of some sort.

One of the most popular forms of holiday with babies and toddlers during the 1950s was the holiday camp. These ranged from the well-known camps like Butlins and Pontins that catered for large numbers of people, to the much smaller, more intimate ones of only a hundred or so holidaymakers. Far less sophisticated than such establishments are now, the camps offered the average working family the opportunity to stay in a well-equipped, if basic by today's standards, chalet, which for the week gave one the privacy of home with the added advantage of having a maid to

Once the baby arrived on the scene, then it was a question of investing in a sidecar to attach to the bike if they wished to continue with days out away from home.

keep it clean and tidy. The large communal dining halls provided three substantial meals each day, but perhaps best of all, entertainment was provided for all the family throughout the day, all included in the one price, except for such luxuries as horse-riding lessons. The babies could be left in the crèche looked after by qualified nursery nurses, while the older children had their own activities club supervised by adults with boundless energy. After the evening meal, mother could settle the children to sleep and when they were, she and father could slip out to join the audience watching first-class entertainment in the theatre and later dance to a live band, happily knowing that patrols round the chalets would alert her if one of the children woke and cried. There were sports facilities and a swimming pool – an indoor heated one in the larger establishments. In fact, there was everything there that one could wish for in a perfect holiday, regardless of the vagaries of the British climate – a bit like facilities offered on the modern cruise.

With all that, it is hardly surprising that gradually many families with small children gave up on the traditional seaside resorts and a week's stay in a boarding house where they were often bound by restrictions and not welcome to be in the house, during the day should the weather be bad. Although there was entertainment to be had at the resort's cinema and theatre, this was not an option with a baby or toddlers. One could take the pushchair into the funfair but that was often noisy and frightening to small children and there was a limit to the number of times you could let your toddler ride on the rather slow roundabout. A wet week at the seaside often meant spending more than the family had intended, frayed tempers and the resolution that next year it was either days out from home or a holiday camp. Luckier were those like Mrs J. who lived in London but had a brother living in Brighton. She and her husband and two little boys could travel by train down to the coast and stay comfortably for several days in the relaxed atmosphere that only close family can give.

11

What to Wear?

*U*nlike inanimate objects that can be ordered in specific sizes and shapes to fit in with your particular requirements, babies at birth have a habit of turning out not to be a standard size. They may be very tiny, long and thin, or short and chubby, and while the aim is for the average of 7 – 7½lb in weight, even that is no guarantee as to the actual shape of the infant. A mother could find herself having to cope with anything from the very small creature that appeared to be in possession of excessively long fingers and feet that overwhelmed the rest of it, through to the 10-pounder that looked as if it had been maturing elsewhere for the previous two months. It was just as well that the 1950s mother only needed vests and nightgowns for the first few weeks of her baby's life, for these could be adapted to fit almost any size. It is to be hoped that in all that earnest knitting that was

Examples of the clothes worn. Note especially the shoes.

taking place amongst her friends and relations, they did not make too many 'first size' matinee jackets and bonnets, for a healthy baby would not need them for long. So when a new mother prepared for her baby she would have been well advised to start following the trend that she herself had grown up with and probably hated, namely making or buying clothes for her baby to 'grow into'. How many mothers must have heaved a deep sigh or even shed a tear when that beautiful little dress or expensive machine-knitted romper suit that was received as gift was discovered to be too small by the time the baby was of a suitable age to wear them.

In the 1950s most mothers were still adhering to the old ideas on suitability. If mothers followed the advice to put the babies outside in the fresh air as much as possible throughout the day, baby would spend most of their first year in what were known as knitted pram suits that consisted of leggings, a jacket-style coat and a bonnet or helmet. The set might also include what were called pilch drawers, that is a pair of knitted pants that covered the nappy and waterproof pants. In warmer weather the leggings would be dispensed with. Most of these garments would have been in traditional colours, white for the very young, progressing to pastel blue for a boy and pink for a girl, as they grew older. In some ways this was a tradition that was continued to some extent by the aftermath of wartime shortages and production restrictions. Once the mills were free to produce wool in many more colours, then some daring mothers opted to dress their infants in pale yellow and turquoise, but only occasionally in green, for some people still retained the superstition that it was unlucky to wear green. One rarely saw baby clothes in other colours but someone had knitted some matinee jackets in bright orange, which they donated to the local hospital. A lovely gesture, but I fear it was a bit tactless of the nursery nurse to dress my newborn, severely jaundiced, niece in one of those garments.

Twenty-first-century mothers have done away with all the fuddy-duddy ideas about baby clothes and, given the wide choice that designers offer them, we often see even very tiny babies wearing what are really scaled–down versions of adult clothes. So very modern, of course, especially for such tiny babes. We won't spoil the present generation's fun by gently reminding them that until the beginning of the twentieth century once a baby had emerged from what were know as 'petti-coats', all their clothes were simply smaller copies of adult wear.

We have already learned elsewhere that once a baby was mobile then overalls or dungarees were the order of the day for playtime. Dresses for baby girls made in a fine material like Vyella or silk or rayon had changed little over the years: they were designed with a yoke and had short puffed sleeves, and invariably the front of the yoke, which was stitched to the gathered skirt, was beautifully embroidered. A simple back opening from the neck allowed the dress to be easily slipped on and off. There was nothing more frightening for a young and inexperienced mother than to discover that she could not get a garment off over the baby's head. It was difficult to stay calm when the infant was scream-ing, its head and ears seemingly growing bigger by the minute. Baby boys wore romper suits, which for the very young ones were just like the little girls' dresses except that they were slightly narrower at the bottom and were fastened at the crutch with press-studs. When going out, a knitted jacket was worn over the romp-ers with leggings and a hat if the weather required it. The average baby, regardless of financial status, rarely had an extensive wardrobe – unless that is, the baby happened to be the recipient of a large number of hand-me-downs from older siblings or cousins. Mollie echoed the situation of many: 'with two small babies and a mortgage we were always hard up. The boys had two romper suits each – one on, the other on the washing line!'

As the baby grew, so too did some of his clothes. Little boys began wearing cotton shirts and little cotton shorts that were attached to a bib, held in place by braces that crossed at the back. Then they progressed to shorts with side buttons. Girls, on the other hand, continued to wear the same style of dress, one set on a yoke, but more likely now to be made of cotton rather than rayon. In winter both sexes wore mainly knitted jumpers and cardigans. As far as underwear was concerned, they both always wore a vest, which might be either hand or machine knitted. Little girls wore petticoats over their vest and plain white knickers, thin cotton in summer, fleecy ones for winter.

Wearing their best coats.

According to some of the '1950s children', they were still wearing liberty bodices, which came between the vest and the petticoat. This was a garment that can best be described as a very slim version of the modern gilet or sleeveless jacket. It was made of a white fleece-lined material that buttoned from just below the neck, down to the hips. It is the buttons that are still remembered by a generation that was brought up on metal, pearl and bone buttons ,because those on the liberty bodice were made of rubber. As little girls grew bigger their bodices also included a rubber button on each side to which, when they were old enough, they would attach the suspenders that would hold up their woollen stockings.

Over all these undergarments, the girl would wear a skirt, possibly knitted, or a kilt and then the jumper and cardigan. This may seem excessive by modern standards but we have to remember that in the 1950s very few houses had central heating, so it was essential to wear layers of clothing to keep the body warm. In most homes, only the main living room was heated so even within the house one needed to keep warm as you moved from room to room. Hence the deep concern by those who advised on early baby care that the temperature of the room in which the baby was should be kept at the correct temperature. In the depth of winter a young child who had been toilet trained for several years might have the occasional accident as a result of putting off having to venture either to the outside lavatory or even to the upstairs bathroom because of the cold.

Once the baby was walking things changed. For a start, he needed shoes. What excitement those first real shoes caused both parents and child, for they marked an extra special milestone in the child's development.

Some time between just under a year and 18 months, most infants will be feeling their feet, quite literally, and will exhibit great delight in showing off to anyone who shows the slightest interest these two magical creations which are attached to their feet. Whether it is the sheer novelty or their usually bright colour, invariably small children draw attention to their shoes. the *Sunday Express Baby Book* recommended that this was the time for the doctor to give the child a physical examination that should include checking legs and feet for any defects that could be easily corrected with the right footwear. If baby's feet and legs were normal, his first shoes should have plenty of toe room, a soft and pliable sole, narrow heels and be shaped like boots with straight sides high enough to give ankle support. Once the child is walking confidently then stronger shoes may be required. Miss Liddiard advised that s h o e s should be of good-quality leather with strong, welted soles, square toes and sufficiently long. She also sensibly advised that mother should examine the shoes and if she noted that the heel of a shoe was worn down on one side she should inform the doctor, 'who would probably order a lift on that side of the heel to be worn for some months to correct the foot that was turning over'. It was quite common in the 1950s to see small children wearing built-up shoes. Shoes at that time were still mostly made of leather; certainly when the original soles and heels on a new pair were worn down, leather was used to repair them. Often it was when a mother took her child's shoes to

Often it was when a mother took her child's shoes to the local cobbler or shoe repair shop that she realised her child's feet needed something to correct the way the shoe was wearing.

the local cobbler or shoe repair shop that she realised her child's feet needed something to correct the way the shoe was wearing.

For many parents the newly walking youngster marked not just a major milestone in the child's development but concern at the cost involved. Parents today still complain about the cost of children's shoes but they do have a much wider choice than was available in the 1950s. At that time the market was dominated by Start-rite, Jumping Jacks and Clarks. Jumping Jacks, which, it was claimed, were designed to give 'ample room for growing toes to wriggle in as well as plenty of good firm support'. started at 24s 6d. Clarks' Play-Ups were similarly designed to play a major part in life-long foot health. Their shoes, they claimed, 'would prevent the bad posture created by ill-fitting shoes'. The fit was described as firm but gentle on the instep and heel, allowing room for toes to grow, while the broad, flexible soles took care of the child's balance. It was that phrase 'room to grow' that caused concern; everyone knew that baby's feet grew quickly and it would not be long before those first shoes that cost 19s 9d would be outgrown and need to be replaced. When the take home pay for many was not much more than £5 one can understand the parental concern. It would seem that Clarks had almost a monopoly on children's shoes and most under 5s wore either their sandals or, in winter, the more solid style which either fastened with a button on the instep, graduating to lace-ups for the boys when they started school. Learning to tie shoelaces was almost another rite of passage; the task of teaching how to tie that bow was often left to father.

To accompany the shoes, there were, of course, socks. These, for small children, were invariably of the ankle variety and were usually white when the child was very small. White continued to be the favoured colour for girls, while boys had either grey or light brown made of machine-knitted cotton that was both washable and hard wearing. By the time the child reached 4 to 5, knee-length knitted woollen socks might be worn, as is shown in the photograph of the brother and sister out with their father. The tops of these were likely to become stretched with wear so they were held in place with garters made of narrow elastic. These home-made bands of what was usually referred to as 'knicker' elastic could also be used to shorten the sleeves of shirts and blouses. When mother bought or received the gift of a hand-me-down garment, it was likely that it was something that had to be 'grown into'. So if the shirt or blouse sleeves ended up covering the child's fingers, mother would place two garters/bands over the sleeve, just above the elbow and then fold over the excess material. Mother could have sewn a tuck in the sleeve, as some did, but the disadvantage to this was that when the sleeves were unstitched sometime later, the material that had been covered up would not necessarily have faded in the same way as the rest of the garment. Incidentally, it was not long before small boys found another use entirely for their garters, when older boys initiated them into the use of makeshift catapults.

Elastic was greatly used in garments in the 1950s. Every little girl who wore a skirt lovingly knitted by mother or grandma would have a piece of elastic threaded through the holes of the waistband.

Elastic was greatly used in garments in the 1950s. Every little girl who wore a skirt lovingly knitted by

We get dressed in our best to go out with dad.

mother or grandma would have a piece of elastic threaded through the holes of the waistband. Similarly her hand-made cotton skirts also had elastic enclosed within the waistband. While this was very good in allowing for the bodily expansion of the child, there came a time when the inevitable happened and the elastic gave way under the strain and broke. This calamity was particularly embarrassing if it should be the elastic in the little girl's knickers. One minute she was walking along, or running in the park, the next she either had the offending garment round her ankles or they had actually tripped her up. One of the many tasks that fell to the 1950s mother was threading new elastic. In garments like knickers, underpants or pyjamas, there was often no way this could be done easily, as the original elastic was enclosed. This meant unpicking the machined stitches of the waistband or, in desperation, making a small hole on the underside (which would have to be darned later) and pulling out what was broken. How to thread in the replacement was the next problem. A tapestry needle or bodkin with an eye wide enough to take the elastic was one way, a small safety pin attached to the end was another, but one commonly used, because every mother could lay her hands on such an object, was to loop the elastic on to a hair clip. Then slowly, it was eased inch-by-inch, through the narrow cavity until it reached the other end. Why bother, asked a child of the 1980s? Because, came the answer, money was short and mothers in the 1950s did not waste anything if they could possibly help it.

Men made shirts last longer by having detachable collars so they at least might be changed daily.

Limited incomes and the relatively high cost of ready-made clothing meant that most people possessed far fewer items of clothing than is usual nowadays. In the days before washing machines were usual, clothes were changed far less frequently; it was still common-place in many families to have a bath at the end of the working week and, having cleaned their body thoroughly, to put on clean under-clothes the following day to last maybe the whole week. Men made shirts last longer

Most houses at that period had sash windows, and in bedrooms the top half was usually pulled down a minimum of 3in.

by having detachable collars so they at least might be changed daily. The dungarees and overalls worn by manual workers and some tradespeople protected their own clothes, while many firms provided uniforms for their staff. In the home most mothers wore an overall or pinafore over a work dress while completing their morning household chores. After lunch they would wash and change into an afternoon dress to take the children out for a walk or to do the shopping. On her return when she set about preparing the evening meal, mother would wear a clean apron, often a pretty one she had made herself from a pattern in *Stitchcraft* maga-zine. In this way she kept her dress or skirt and jumper clean and at the same time, in accordance with the advice given in women's magazines, made herself look attractive for when father came home. Children, too, wore aprons to keep their clothes clean while they were playing, tabards for boys and pinafores for the girls.

Children had little say in what they wore. Mother bought or made their clothes and it was she who decreed what they would wear. Since the supply was

limited, there would have been little to choose from
had the option been there. As it was, unless the clothes
were too soiled to be worn the following day, when the
child undressed at night his clothes would have been
carefully hung up in his cupboard, or folded up and
placed on the chair in his bedroom or at the foot of the
bed. Many 1950s children can testify to the fact that
their mothers adhered to the advice they had received
and made sure that their child slept in a well-ventilated
bedroom. Most houses at that period had sash windows, and in bedrooms the top half was usually pulled
down a minimum of 3in. Some mothers insisted on
the bottom window being raised the same amount to
create a good circulation of fresh air. This was acceptable in high summer temperatures but in the depths
of winter was unendurable. No central heating, no
carpet on the floor, only cold linoleum and often no
hot-water bottle:

> We had lino throughout the house with the odd rug
> on the floor, only one fire in the living room and no
> heating anywhere else. It was very cold in the winter
> months. My brother and I would bath in front of the
> fire – lovely. The sheets on my bed sometimes felt
> really cold. I was convinced they were still wet from
> being washed.

So wrote Colleen. It is no wonder that as they got older
and were not supervised as they got ready for bed,
some children would keep their vests on under their
nightwear, and their socks too, while others put their
underclothes under the pillow so that they would be
warm to put on in the morning.

Faced with old, undated family photographs, one of
the best ways of being able to put a rough estimate as

to when it was taken is to look at the children's coats. The 1950s were the heyday for those smart double-breasted tweed coats, sometimes with an inset of velvet on the collar worn by most small boys at the time. A very young Prince Charles was spotted wearing one and soon Marks and Spencer was leading the way in making similar ones available at an affordable price. It did not matter if your child's version of the coat had come from one of the expensive London stores or the local Co-operative store, your little boy was in the fashion, as both the photograph to which we referred earlier and the one showing the two little boys visiting Father Christmas show. Marks and Spencer was now quickly becoming the department store where families of modest income shopped.

Fine corduroy was also popular for little girls' coats. To accompany the coat there was often a matching hat in the same material: a cap for the boys that was slightly boxier than a school cap, for the girls a bonnet.

Although the contributors to this work came from very varied backgrounds, only one declared that she never shopped there. The photograph of the brother and sister shows the type of coat little girls were wearing. Theirs tended to be shaped at the waist and were made of fine woollen cloth usually in a plain colour. Fine corduroy was also popular for little girls' coats. To accompany the coat there was often a matching hat in the same material: a cap for the boys that was slightly boxier than a school cap, for the girls a bonnet. If the coat came without a matching hat, then mother would buy – or knit – a pixie hood for her little daughter and a helmet for her son.

Following the austerity of the war years and the ones that came immediately after, mothers were able to indulge their children slightly by decorating their jumpers and cardigans with designs that varied from

Best coats, too, for meeting Father Christmas.

animals like baby rabbits, toys such as miniature ted-
dies and sailing ships to seaside items like sea shells and
star fish – whatever happened to be the pattern of the
month in *Stitchcraft* or one of the women's magazines.
They could make knitted bathing costumes or sew sun
dresses; they could make fancy-dress costumes: pirates
and cowboys, nurses and fairies, or even as in the
case of one little boy, make him a Pearly King outfit
to wear for the fancy dress parade on the day of the
Coronation. One can imagine his mother raiding her
own and everyone else's button boxes (do these still
exist?) to find sufficient amounts of those little pearl
buttons that once graced delicate clothes. In those days,
mothers could, and were expected to, turn their hands
to making everything.

Certainly shops sell-
ing fancy-dress clothes
such as that depicted
much later in the chil-
dren's TV programme
Mr Benn were few and
far between.

> *Regardless of the religious motive
> for attending Sunday services, it
> has to be acknowledged that going
> to church often gave people a chance
> to put on their best clothes.*

The 1950s mother
took it as a matter of
course that once the
little ones were in bed, she would relax and listen to
the wireless with her knitting in hand. This was not
regarded as just another chore for many it was a
satisfying hobby. Women seemed to have relished
experimenting with the wide variety of wools that
were appearing in the shops. Angora was one that
enjoyed great popularity in the 1950s. If one had
a little girl then it was a delight to make her a fluffy
white or pink bolero to go over her best party frock.
'Best' clothes, too, were still very much a feature of life

in the 1950s, for adults as well as children. When one bought a new coat, dress or suit, it was worn initially only on Sundays or for special occasions. It is difficult now to explain to those who are too young to remember just how different Sunday used to be to the rest of the week. Colleen noted:

> Sunday was observed as a special day by my Mum and we had to wear our 'good' clothes and stay clean and keep to our back garden. We weren't allowed to play with other children because it was Sunday! We occasionally visited Nana and she always did apple pie and custard, which I really enjoyed. Roast chicken was a special Sunday meal.

Colleen does not mention if she attended Sunday School before the age of 5, or if she was taken to church by her parents. Regardless of the religious motive for attending Sunday services, it has to be acknowledged that going to church often gave people a chance to put on their best clothes. In some parts of the country the custom still persisted of having new clothes which appeared for the first time in church on Whit Sunday. In some places, a new hat, rather than an Easter egg (unobtainable anyway during sweet rationing) celebrated the coming of Easter and the spring. Sunday was officially a day of rest, so apart from attending church twice or possibly three times during the day, there was nothing else to do. So, as Colleen suggested, families visited each other; they cooked a good Sunday roast dinner and they followed that up with a good brisk Sunday afternoon walk for the whole family. If the weather was too inclement then children were expected to play quietly with their toys or to look at books. This might be the time that parents introduced them to simple board or card games such as snap or happy families. For small children Sundays always felt longer than any other day of the week and it was a relief to take off their best clothes at the end of the day and know that tomorrow they would go back to the old routine.

A Pearly King for the Queen's Coronation.

Let's play ball.

12

Mother's 'Me' Time

Young women of the 1950s regarded themselves as much more modern in their outlook
than their mothers and, once the restraints that
wartime conditions had imposed were lifted, many
believed that they would not only achieve equality
with men in the workplace but they would also gain
the freedom to enjoy a full social life. That was true
for the single, working girl – to some extent. There
was still, however, male disapproval of women entering public houses unaccompanied by a male, and even
restaurants tended to seat a lone woman at a table in
the most secluded part of the room. Was it purely her
imagination that a young woman on her own was
made to feel that she was a threat? If she booked into
a hotel by herself she was often made to feel that her
motives for doing so were being treated with suspicion.
As for attending parties, she might find herself discuss-

ing business with male colleagues but across the room their wives were eyeing her every gesture with distrust. So, if the single woman really wanted to enjoy her leisure time she needed to find a friend in a similar position.

The single woman might have hours at her disposal which she needed to fill with leisure or social activities, but what of those young married women who had become mothers? By the end of the twentieth century it had become customary to hear women talking about 'Me' time. Encouraged by magazines and TV programmes, they expected to be able to leave their children in the care of their husbands or partners and take off for a pampering weekend at a spa hotel or a trip to Paris or some other European city for shopping and nightclubs. The more athletic might join a group of friends for a walking tour; the creative ones for sessions in quilting or dressmaking – the choice seems endless but the end is the same, it is a break from everyday routine and a chance for the woman to express what she might call 'the real me'.

One can almost hear the audible harrumphing of those who were housewives and mothers in the 1950s and the muttered, 'it wasn't like that in our day'. Of course it wasn't! But it might surprise them to know that many of the 1950s magazines and books of advice did indeed advocate that mothers should have some 'Me' time. The phrase was actually used occasionally

Once the novelty of the baby had worn off somewhat, the reality of being at home all day, with all that the domestic life entailed, could result in many women looking back to the carefree days before baby had placed such restrictions on her life.

but it was most likely to apply to the woman making the opportunity to have a slightly longer than usual time in the bath. One, that is, by herself with some nice-smelling bath salts rather than with one or two of her children for company. Young mothers were urged to keep themselves looking good for their husbands, to apply beauty products, most of which they could not afford; in fact, when it boiled down to it, most of the advice was aimed at keeping their men folk happy rather than pleasing the women themselves. It was a recognised fact that the months immediately following the arrival of a baby could be difficult for a couple. Most of the woman's time and energy was absorbed with the baby and it needed a very well-adjusted couple to deal with any feelings the husband might have of neglect or being sidelined. Understandably, the new father might seek refuge from drying nappies or a 'colicky' infant by going for a pint at his local, and then stopping to play a game of darts. If this became a regular occurrence then resentment could build up on the part of the new mother and relations between them would be strained.

A letter to the problem page of a magazine told of a young mother's feeling of neglect as well as loneliness. Her husband worked all day, then, presumably in an attempt to better his chances of promotion or to pursue a different career, he attended night school three evenings a week and on the other two he played badminton. She said she did not grudge him his pleasure (though she obviously did!) as he always helped her in the house and garden at the weekend, but each evening she sat alone and remembered the good times she had had before she married. She now lived a long way from her old home and felt so lonely. Sweet girl that she must have been, she confessed at the end of her letter that she felt wicked for being so discontented.

Would anyone in similar circumstances nowadays refer to themselves as wicked? The lady dispensing advice assured her she was nothing of the kind, but it was not healthy for her to spend so long on her own. Sensibly, rather in the mode of 'keeping a stiff upper lip and pulling herself together', the woman was told it was up to her to do something about changing the situation. First she needed to talk about her feelings to her husband. The advisor did volunteer the comment that she thought the husband was a bit thoughtless not to give her his company on at least one night a week. On the practical side it was suggested that she should invite some of the neighbours in for the evening and if she found there was one whom she felt she could thoroughly trust, then perhaps she could leave the baby with her while she too joined an evening class that interested her.

What a great institution those evening classes were in the 1950s through to the 1970s. Not only did they give individuals the chance to improve their academic education or develop skills in subjects as diverse as pottery and motor mechanics, they also proved an excellent way to widen one's social circle and make new friends, often from a very different background. It also became a standing joke that most magazine agony aunts recommended evening classes as one of the best ways for a single woman to meet a man. How disappointing when one discovered that the class members of the woodturning or 'know the inside of a car' were predominantly female!

Returning to our letter writer, she did represent a very large number of women in similar circumstances. Once the novelty of the baby had worn off somewhat, the reality of being at home all day, with all that the domestic life entailed, could result in many women looking back to the carefree days before baby had placed such restrictions on her life. No longer could she and her husband have a quick count up of the loose change in their coat pockets to see if they had enough to take themselves to the cinema. Even if they had more than enough, they could not go because of the baby. If they lived close to family, then parents or younger sisters could be prevailed upon to come and listen out for the baby. If the infant was still at the carrycot stage, then it could be taken and left with the grandparents for the evening. That way they did not have to exchange the comfort of their own living room, perhaps with a television set, for the sparsely furnished home of the young couple. Those who did not live near close family or friends had to rely on others. Jean reported that girls from the typing pool in her husband's office would sit with her baby in return for a snack supper and perhaps a box of chocolates. Others offered a young student the opportunity to have a chance to study for two or three hours away from crowded home conditions, although that relied on the baby sleeping peacefully during the parents' absence. Similarly a courting couple would often jump at the chance to have uninterrupted time together, while sensible people like Mrs SJ made sure that the 'nice young woman to whom she rented a bed-sitter would be more than happy to listen out for the baby while she marked a stack of exercise books'. Babysitting had yet to become a business!

However, in the case of our letter writer, she was one of those who no longer had family members within

There was also the opportunity just to chat or exchange recipes and ideas.

easy distance. When she felt lonely and depressed she could not put the baby in its pram and walk a few streets away to have a cup of tea with mum or grandma or visit with old school friends and their young families. One of the biggest drawbacks to the local authority building programmes in the late 1940s and early 1950s was that, while they quite rightly concentrated on building homes, the other facilities which would provide opportunities for people to meet together were the last to come. It is a pity that our lonely letter writer did not live on the prefab estate featured in another letter that appeared in *Mother* magazine in 1951.

This described how, as each family moved into their new prefabricated bungalow with all its most up-to-date conveniences, those already in residence made a point of greeting them. It was a chance remark by a young woman that she wished there was a club to which she could go occasionally to meet others and have discussions that gave the correspondent the idea to invite about a dozen of her neighbours to her home one evening to sound them out about the possibility of starting their own club. Her invitation included the advice to bring a chair! The idea was enthusiastically received and by the end of the evening they had chosen a secretary and treasurer and decided upon the most suitable day of the week for their meetings. It seemed 7.30 was the most suitable time for them: the evening meal would be finished, babies and very young children were put to bed while the older ones would be engrossed in their various hobbies or homework, and dad would look after them. It was also agreed that members would take it in turns to hold the meetings in their homes. Just as in a properly regulated clubs an annual membership fee was set at 2s 6d. A weekly fee of 1s was also charged. From that money, every sixth week the group had enough to pay for them to visit the local theatre or the cinema. Any money left after paying for the tickets was put into a kitty, which mounted up and could later be drawn on to pay for a gift for the occasional visiting speakers they had. These varied widely from the local hairdresser giving a beauty demonstration or a specialist giving craft instruction, but also included talks by a representative of the Marriage Guidance Council, the Local Government Health Inspector, the Red Cross and the editor of the local newspaper. None of the speakers expected a fee, but received instead either a posy of flowers or a packet of cigarettes, whichever was considered appropriate.

Some weeks they had a debate or discussion on topics that were relevant at the time, followed by a games evening. There was also the opportunity just to chat or exchange recipes and ideas. In time they developed their own circle of those who were willing to babysit for others, out of which grew a network of those willing and able to give practical help when needed, such as meeting a child from school when mother had just had a new baby, or shopping or cleaning when someone was ill. Strangely, they called themselves the Hen Club but the main thing was that one woman had had the initiative to fulfil a need that provided, in her words, fun and laughter as well as companionship and a sense that they were not alone. Informal groups such as the Hen Club, began to flourish throughout

Many rural women had never known the luxury of electricity for lighting and cooking, or turning on a tap above the sink; instead they were still having to fetch their water from a communal well or a pump in the yard.

the country and have continued to do so wherever there are women who feel the need for the comradeship of others like them.

Of course there were already well-established groups for women. The Anglican Church offered membership of the Mothers' Union to married members of the congregation, while most of the Nonconformist churches had similar organisations. These tended to be afternoon meetings that gave members an opportunity to learn more about missionary work overseas, perhaps from a visiting speaker. That might lead to the group undertaking either fund raising for the mission or engaging in more practical work like knitting or sewing garments for babies in Africa or India. The meeting would end with a cup of tea and the chance to chat. These meetings could be a most welcome break in the routine of the young mother, as often the group provided supervision for their babies and toddlers in another room. Again, all arrangements were made by the members themselves; the kind ladies who kept an eye on the children for a couple of hours had had no training, only their own past experience, and certainly had not been vetted by the police as to their suitability, but then neither had the church or chapel meeting room been subject to a risk assessment or health and safety check. When one thinks back to some of the locations used, one can now see dangers that were either unrecognised or totally disregarded at that time.

Women living in rural areas had the opportunity to join the monthly meetings of the Women's Institute (WI). We need to remember that in the 1950s the rural population was made up almost entirely of those involved in some way with agriculture. Farmers were still employing men to do the work that has nowadays

been entirely taken over by machinery. These workers
and their families lived in cottages, which were tied in
with their employment. Their wives were often roped
in to help with casual work in the fields, especially
at harvest time. If the farmer ran a dairy herd, local
women might find work for themselves in the dairy,
bottling the milk for local rounds or making cheese
and butter. Many rural women had never known the
luxury of electricity for lighting and cooking, or turning on a tap above the sink; instead they were still
having to fetch their water from a communal well or
a pump in the yard. As for bathing, that was done in a
zinc bath in front of the living room fire on Saturday
night, while going to the lavatory involved a visit
either to a lean-to shed in the yard or a rough cor-
rugated iron-roofed wooden shed some distance from
the house that contained either an earth closet with a
scrubbed wooden seat and a bottom-sized hole in it or,
if one's landlord was more modern, an Elsan chemical toilet. However, to make up for what was lacking,
the countrywoman was very much a part of a united
community. She might spend her day in old jumpers
and skirts, and need to wear her wellies as she went
about her chores feeding chickens and pigs or gathering vegetables from the garden, but come WI night it
was a very different story. This, probably apart from
Sunday, was the only chance she had to dress up and
be herself. This was her 'Me' time. Most villages had
their own WI hall, some more splendid than others.
Many dated from the early 1920s, constructed of cor-
rugated iron usually painted green; they were erected
as very practical war memorials. Over the years the
interior walls were lined and a kitchen was either
carved out of the original hut or an extension was
built on to accommodate it. Similarly an earth closet,

later replaced by a chemical toilet, was housed out the back.

The village at that period still had its own hierarchy. If it had managed to survive being commandeered by the military then the manor or big house might once again be occupied by the largest landowner, who might still be referred to as the squire. The next largest house was probably the rectory or vicarage, for in those days each parish still had its own clergyman. Several other houses dating from the very early nineteenth century might house those who were known in the village as 'the gentry'; the retired military colonels and captains, or their widows; plus the elderly spinster daughters of tradesmen from the town who had made their fortune and moved to the country to enjoy the results of their labour. Then there were the small farmers and the professional people like the doctor, the head teacher of the village school, the blacksmith, the miller, the publicans and shopkeepers. Although in the 1950s people were still conscious of the differences in class and status it was the proud boast of the WI that its members came from all classes, that they 'were sisters the moment they entered the institute room whether duchess or sweeper's wife, they were out to help and encourage each other'. regardless of religious or political beliefs.

Apart from providing much-needed companionship and a break from the home, the WI encouraged countrywomen to widen their experiences of life.

It was perhaps inevitable that even in the 1950s it was 'the lady from the big house' or the rector's wife who was president, for she, after all, had more time than the working women and was accustomed to getting things done, but the wife of the shepherd could be the secretary or treasurer. Apart from providing much-needed companionship and a break from the home, the WI encouraged countrywomen to widen their experiences of life. They were challenged to achieve the best they could in the domestic arts with which they were familiar, as well as developing talents they might not realise they had. Becoming part of the choir gave women an opportunity, literally, to let their voice be heard and even a very shy young woman might be encouraged to take a small part in a play. There was a great deal more to the WI than simply Jam and Jerusalem. The nickname came about during the war when the movement was called upon by the government, not only to pick every available fruit possible that could be turned into preserves but for each group to get together actually to make jam to help feed the troops. The spirit continued and the WI members could be relied upon to be in the front line to help out in any local crisis.

In 1950 the WI petitioned the government that parents should be allowed to visit their children in hospital.

At national level, the movement was not afraid to make its voice heard and each year at its annual meeting it would present resolutions to the government. Each of these would have been thoroughly discussed throughout the land in even the smallest institute, making every member feel that she was able to make her voice heard on important issues. In 1950 the WI petitioned the government that parents should be allowed to visit their children in hospital. It may come as a shock to today's mothers to learn that in those far-off days of the 1950s if your child was taken into hospital for any reason, then both you and your child were parted until the child was discharged. As a child who experienced this, I can testify to how frightening it was to be suddenly taken into a huge ward and placed in an iron bedstead where one remained all day except on the day of the operation. To this day I can recall being wheeled into the operating theatre, and as the mask was placed over my mouth, I begged to see my mother. The whole episode was enough to create a fear of hospitals. Later, as a mother who was allowed to stay night and day with my own child in hospital, I realise how hard it must have been for my mother and all those who were not allowed to see their children, even during normal visiting hours.

The Co-operative Women's Guild grew out of the suffrage movement and was firmly rooted in the Labour movement.

For the Festival of Britain in 1951 the WI featured their model house for the working family. A lovely rural touch to this modern house was the inclusion of a porch for muddy boots. With a house like that, the 1950s housewife would not have to put up with dirty footmarks on her kitchen floor nor would her husband be forced into leaving his boots by the back door. As a follow up to the dream of modern housing for farm workers, in 1952 the government was asked to speed up the provision of electricity in rural areas. Four years later the movement was expressing its deep concern over the impact of the withdrawal of rail and bus services in the country.

The Townswomen's Guild (TWG) was not intended as an urban answer to the WI. Formed in 1929, its aim was to encourage an understanding and interest in world citizenship in women, but within three or four years it decided to concentrate on education rather than politics. By the 1950s the TWG was making its voice heard as members took the government to task on matters of national importance. Basically, however, its aims have become those of most groups for women to offer a place where they may discuss their ideas and opinions, learn new skills, support their fellow members, make friends and, above all, have fun. The Co-operative Women's Guild grew out of the suffrage movement and was firmly rooted in the Labour movement. It seemed much more serious in its objectives by concentrating on campaigns for equal pay, for example, and issues that particularly concerned working class women. Its emphasis was on providing educational opportunities for women who had missed out at school. It is likely that membership increased among younger women during the early 1950s, when many young mothers found themselves on the newly built estates, which, without shops initially, were served by the individual mobile Co-op vans, which brought milk, bread, grocery, greengrocery, meat and coal to their door. Most women found it sensible to buy their £1 share in the Co-op, especially as they were buying most of their weekly shopping from them, and the twice-yearly dividend was a godsend to many families in helping to buy the children's new shoes or winter coats. Another advantage was that the share was held in the wife's name, so only she could collect the dividend, not her husband.

As the 1950s progressed many women became more militant in their attitudes.

All these groups gave women their 'Me' time – the friendship, relaxation and fun – but many discovered that this 'Me' time developed their personalities and gave them both confidence and fulfilment in a way they had never expected. From taking a leading part in their local clubs, they often went on to become committee members at county and national level. Others entered local politics as councillors, a few even becoming Members of Parliament. As the 1950s progressed many women became more militant in their attitudes, leading the way to their supporting not only the emerging feminist movement but also throwing themselves into the CND (Campaign for Nuclear Disarmament). Some mothers felt so strongly that they had to fight for a world free of the threat of war that they would, in the 1980s, even be prepared to face the hardships of the camp on Greenham Common.

13

Childhood Illnesses

*T*he young mother in the 1950s had to be pre-pared to face the multitude of ailments and mishaps that might befall her child. And while she could always fall back on the local clinic for advice rather than calling in the doctor, there were some things she needed to be prepared to deal with at home. To that end she was advised to keep a nurs-ery medical cupboard such as the one suggested in *You and Your Baby*, a publication issued by the Nestlé Company. What would mothers of the second decade of the twenty-first century make of some of the items that in the 1950s were considered to be essential? At first sight, the modern reader might be forgiven for thinking that this list is culinary rather than medi-cal, since it includes several of the ingredients for making mayonnaise:

```
Boracic powder or crystals.    Packet of white lint.
Small jar of common salt.      Packet of boracic or pink
Small jar of zinc ointment.    lint.
4oz bottle of castor oil.      1 tin of Antiphlogistine.
4oz bottle of olive oil.       Elastoplast.
4oz tin of mustard.            Bandages.
2oz bottle of friar's
balsam.
Roll of cotton wool.
```

A solution of salt is a simple and effective antiseptic that speeds the healing process, particularly if used in a hot bath. Olive oil (which was very expensive at the time) was used specifically in the care of premature babies but more generally to treat mild earache. The bowl of a small spoon was warmed for a few seconds in boiling water, then drops of oil were poured into it and these were then slowly dripped into the painful ear. A small plug of cotton wool was then placed in the outer ear to keep it warm. As for the mustard, that was used with the ratio of one dessert-spoonful of mustard powder to every gallon of bath water. For generations, a baby suffering from convulsions would be placed in a warm mustard bath.

'The children with adenoids are always mouth breathers and a little deaf; this gives them a vacant, stupid expression, and they are usually very backward at school.'

Mustard footbaths were also recommended as a measure against colds. A child caught in a rainstorm who came home soaked to the skin was likely to find himself stripped and put into clean, warm clothing and made to sit with his feet in a bowl of the mustard solution.

Boracic crystals – one teaspoonful to 1 pint of boiled (not boiling) water – could be used as a mild antiseptic for bathing eyes and other areas that could not bear a saline solution. Mixed with glycerine it could be used too as a mouth wash or a gargle. Boracic lint was used to make fomentations for conditions such as boils and septic wounds. Zinc and castor ointment was every mother's friend when it came to baby's chafed or sore buttocks. As for the dreaded castor oil, which was usually given as a purgative, its use with children was not advised except on doctor's orders. It could, however, also be used warm, as drops to treat irritations of the eyes. Drops of the bright yellow friar's balsam, placed in a bowl of steaming water, were used as an inhalant to relieve nasal and chest congestion. The impressive sounding antiphlogistine is better known as kaolin, which was used to make poultices to reduce inflammation.

Having assembled her absolute necessities, the new mother would be wary of anything that might be amiss with her child. The books told her that listlessness, bad temper, loss of appetite and heavy eyes were sure signs that baby was not feeling well. How, she might wonder, was she to recognise what was listlessness as opposed to just being tired and did bad temper mean that the baby was crying more than usual? The book suggested that indigestion, teething or a cold might be the reason – or it might be something more serious, in which case, the doctor should be consulted. It is interesting to note that of the things that might be wrong, there is no mention of meningitis of which we hear today. Instead there is an alphabetical list that runs from adenoids to worms, taking in bowel movements and flat feet on the way.

The 1930s and 1940s seemed to regard tonsils and adenoids as being responsible for many childhood problems and therefore they should be got rid of as soon as possible.

In the 1930s, children were often subjected to tonsillectomy, not in hospital but performed by the GP on the kitchen table. The wholesale removal of Ts & As, as they were known in the 1940s, meant that regularly thirty or so children at a time spent a week in their local hospital for the operation. The Nestlé book mentions that the abnormal growths known as adenoids block the air passages behind the nostrils and may be caused in the

'That child must have worms', was a common expression, usually voiced by grandparents or elderly aunts to describe a small child with a large appetite.

very early days after birth by keeping the baby in a hot, dry atmosphere due to bad ventilation. In other words, if your child had adenoids it was your fault. As one might expect, *The Mothercraft Manual* is even blunter, coming up with the sweeping and hurtful statement: 'The children with adenoids are always mouth breathers and a little deaf; this gives them a vacant, stupid expression, and they are usually very backward at school.' It was also believed that adenoids caused a child to be listless, with a loss of appetite and susceptible to illness. Any child who failed to put on weight was treated with suspicion and was thus a candidate for the removal of adenoids. Incidentally, primary schoolchildren who weighed more than the average were similarly treated. There was a further fear that the unhealthy tissue was a breeding ground for tubercular germs, a disease that was finally on the decrease. So with all these fears where adenoids were concerned it was a question of better out than in. However, by the end of the 1950s medical opinion had decided that tonsils did indeed serve a useful purpose and the automatic removal of Ts & As was dropped.

Under the heading of enlarged glands there is a dire warning. Since the glands are not specified we must assume that they refer to those in the neck, behind the ears and under the arm. These swellings, we are told, may denote the child is 'run down' but they may also be the result of 'infected tonsils, decayed teeth or verminous conditions'. A contributor who had her tonsils removed at the age of 6 went on to suffer throughout her teens and twenties with sore throats and swollen neck glands. She was eventually told that her condition was caused by the lack of those tonsils, which would have been able to fight her throat infections! But what of decayed teeth and vermin? Just what had the mother to look forward to once her child had finally acquired teeth and then came into contact with other children who might pass on … who knew what? The prospects were frightening but thank goodness for the nurses at the clinic and the friendly health visitor who could reassure rather than frighten.

About an inch in length, threadworms look just like pieces of cotton.

'That child must have worms', was a common expression, usually voiced by grandparents or elderly aunts to describe a small child with a large appetite. The healthy toddler who had exerted a great deal of energy racing round the park or garden would often consume rather more bread and butter or cake than was thought suitable by his elderly relations who had forgotten that it was perfectly natural. However, these worms they talked of must have been a very real part of life at that time if we are to judge by the advertisements which appeared in both women's magazines and those specifically dedicated to mothers and babies. For example we have:

Flowerdells Ltd.- Dual active tablets which:
- eliminate the worm completely;
- build up the body's resistance to further infection;
- do not cause any biliousness or colic;
- are very pleasant to take.
- No 1 Tablets for children under 7.
- No 2 Tablets for children over 7 and adults.
- Price 2s 5½d and 15s 0d – postage 4d.

Ask your chemist to obtain them for you.

There were three types of worms that were likely to infest the intestines of young children: threadworms, roundworms and tapeworms. Their presence could cause general indigestion, irritability, restlessness and nightmares, and the most telling, itching around the anus. About an inch in length, threadworms look just like pieces of cotton. Certainty of the condition came when the worms, which lay eggs, were actually seen wriggling in the child's faeces. Unfortunately children often re-infected them-selves by scratching their bottoms and get-ting the eggs under their fingernails. If hands were not washed carefully the eggs were then transferred to their

Spots that appeared behind the ear were also associated with head lice.

food. Hygiene is therefore of paramount importance as it is possible to infect the whole household if, for exam-ple, the infected child sleeps either with a sibling or in its parents' bed where eggs had been deposited on the sheets. This accounts for why Flowerdells Ltd offered tablets for adults as well as for children. Roundworms are almost white and in size and formation very similar to earthworms but there were rarely more than two present in the child. The single tapeworm not only made the sufferer very ill, it was also much more difficult to deal with. Since it had a segmented body, only parts of it passed through the patient and only when the head had finally been excreted could the child be declared free. In the meantime the child lost not only energy but weight too. Was it just an urban myth that pills containing tapeworm eggs were sold as a slimming aid in the 1950s?

Not to be confused with the above worms was ringworm. This highly contagious condition comes under the general heading of skin complaints and could occur on both the scalp and body of very young babies, forming circles of horny scales. In severe cases the hair became thin and bald patches appeared. Like scabies, a disease that caused intense irritation, it was caused by a parasite attacking the skin. Both conditions were highly contagious and took a long time to clear, requiring scrupulous cleansing of clothing and bedding. In extreme cases disinfecting and fumigation might be required, which involved taking all the infested bedding to the Local Authority Cleansing Station. Most mothers would not have had to worry about either of these but those who were forced to live in overcrowded housing with poor sanitary arrangements needed to be warned of the possibilities.

Those who had the luxury of their own house might well turn the little-used front room into a temporary sickroom.

Other nasty ailments that could befall a child included the contagious skin disease known as impetigo. Children, who have a habit of putting things they ought not into their mouths, were told that sucking pennies could cause this, presumably because of the red spots that appeared on the face and around the mouth in particular. In reality it was caught from another child who was already infected. Spots that appeared behind the ear were also associated with head lice. However, those associated with impetigo soon turned moist and then developed a yellow crust. To make matters even more colourful, treatment, once the crusts had formed, was bathing the infected parts with warm oil or boracic lotion and then applying the antiseptic known as gentian violet. Once that awful colour had been applied, the child must have felt like a medieval leper as mothers pulled their children away from any contact.

It was as well that the mother should be prepared for all eventualities, but on the whole it was likely that the most she would have to deal with were the usual childhood illnesses. The conscientious mother of the 1950s would have taken advantage of all the inoculations and vaccinations against these which were available for her child. They did not necessarily mean the child would not catch measles, whooping cough or whatever, but if he did it was likely to be a very mild dose.

The table below shows, among other things, how long the period of quarantine was at that time. Often this was taken quite literally and the child was kept isolated in one room. Those who had the luxury of their own house might well turn the little-used front room into a temporary sickroom. While this seemed a very sensible solution, it had its drawbacks as one mother found to her cost when she discovered that her little daughter, bored with looking at books and doing jigsaws, had decided to 'help mummy' by polishing the whole piano with calamine lotion.

Disease	Incubation Period	Appearance of Rash	Quarantine	Patient Contacts
Scarlet Fever	1–8 days	1–2 days	14 days	7 days
Diphtheria	2–10 days	14–21 days	10–14 days	
Measles	7–14 days	4 days	21 days	21 days (infants)
German Measles	5–11 days	0–2 days	7 days	21 days (infants)
Mumps	12–14 days	7 days after swelling has subsided	None	
Whooping Cough	6–18 days	6 weeks from commencement	6 weeks (infants only)	
Chicken Pox	11–21 days	0–2 days	21 days, or until all scabs have disappeared	21 days
Smallpox	10–14 days	3 days	6 weeks	16 days, unless recently vaccinated

Unlike those childhood illnesses which feature spots of various types, whooping cough starts with what at first seems to be several days of persistent coughing. However, it quickly develops into the recognisable paroxysms that usually end in bouts of vomiting. Often it is the starting of a meal that causes the coughing fit so that after a time the child refuses to take food. Bed rest in a warm but well-ventilated room free of draughts was considered essential. The various manuals all said that the doctor attending the child would supervise the special treatment necessary. Since the coughing fits could last between six and eight weeks, mothers would no doubt have become anxious that the child was not getting enough nourishment, especially as the child grew visibly thinner. This was a problem that had faced a Mrs Woolhurst of Sheffield. She shared details of how she had overcome it in a letter to *Mother* magazine in January 1951. Her 3-year-old had vomited her food for a fortnight and then refused all food. Her doctor had said the child must eat or she would have to go into hospital (where presumably she would have been fed intravenously). A chance conversation with a woman who had an interest in diets used in sickness produced the following. First, the mother was to remove all starches (bread and potatoes) and milk, fat, eggs, meat and fish from the child's daily foods. This left her asking what on earth she could give her little daughter. The answer was:

<u>On rising:</u> Fruit juice.

<u>Breakfast:</u> Apple muesli (soak a tablespoon of raw porridge oats in water over night); next morning grate a medium sized apple into the oats, adding a little honey or a few raisins;
or grated raw apple and crispbread with a scrape of butter;
or half a grapefruit.

<u>Lunch:</u> Tomato or vegetable soup, green or root vegetables with grated cheese or milled nuts; baked or stewed apple with honey.

<u>Tea:</u> Raw mixed salad with crispbread; fruit juice or water to drink.

Mrs Woolhurst reported that once the little girl was induced to try this regime she ceased vomiting when she whooped. The diet was continued until the coughing stopped and the child was 'as lively as a cricket'. This is in fact a variation of a slimming diet popular amongst the wealthy in the 1930s. What readers may find interesting is the use of the term 'muesli', which most of us associate with its commercial introduction in the late 1960s. It just goes to show that the 1950s were not as behind the times as we thought!

Who now remembers the inspiring story of the life and work of the Australian nurse Sister Kenny that was turned into a film? She it was who came up with a radical treatment for a disease which throughout history had had a crippling effect, quite literally, on young children. Known by an assortment of different names, mothers of the 1950s would have grown up having seen those who had suffered and survived this frightening disease. Before the introduction of the Salk vaccine in the 1950s many of those who were diagnosed as suffering from infantile paralysis were, as the name suggests, paralysed partially or wholly. The

A mass immunisation of all children immediately took place and then the schools were closed for an extra long summer holiday.

really bad cases were consigned to being incarcerated in a machine, somewhat similar to the modern body scanner, which took over the control of the body's functions. This frightening machine, known as the iron lung, featured in several romantic films of the late 1940s and early 1950s, which did little to lessen the public's fears. Then in 1954 there was a very severe outbreak of the disease in the United Kingdom. The illness had always been associated in the past with hot weather and insanitary conditions, so when cases were reported throughout the country it was believed that outdoor public swimming pools were responsible for its spread. Consequently most of them were closed during the heat wave. Teacher Mrs G recalled the outbreak in Suffolk in the summer of 1954. Children began falling ill with flu-like symptoms just before the end of the school year. A mass immunisation of all children immediately took place and then the schools were closed for an extra long summer holiday. They did not reopen until the beginning of the new term. Mrs G never found out what happened to John, the little boy from her class who contracted the disease, because the new term brought a new class for her, but she believes that when he did return to school he walked with a limp.

There was also a mild panic when it was believed that it was possible to catch the disease through drinking directly from a bottle. At that time all schoolchildren were given a third of a pint of milk during their morning break. The bottles they came in were sealed with a cap and each child was supposed to use the straws the school provided. Unfortunately, the 'straws' were not always made of straw but of thick paper and

The compulsory free vaccination against smallpox introduced in the nineteenth century meant that this was another disease that had almost been eradicated.

these could sometimes deflate, making sucking very difficult. The impatient child would dispense with it, and drink straight from the bottle as some of them did from lemonade bottles. It is possible that inadequate cleansing at the bottling plant was responsible for an outbreak of some sort; most likely it would have been what is now identified as E. coli. The work on developing a vaccine against the crippling childhood disease came too late for those who suffered its ill effects in the 1954 outbreak, but when the Salk vaccine did become available, mothers made sure that their babies were vaccinated against what we now refer to as poliomyelitis because it was discovered that the disease no longer attacked only very young children, schoolchildren and young adults were vulnerable too. Another teacher who remembered an outbreak of polio in the late 1950s was among the younger members of staff who were inoculated along with all the pupils in the grammar school. She recalls the great buzz of excitement as the girls tried to find out which of their teachers were 25 and under. However, it was reassuring for adults to know that protection was being offered to them too.

There was now protection too against that other scourge of the past, tuberculosis. The introduction of the BCG vaccination for babies and young children provided them with immunity against this dreaded lung disease, while adults, particularly those who worked in professions which brought them into close contact with the general public, were subject to regular chest X-rays aimed to detect any signs of the disease so that they could receive immediate treatment. The mobile X-ray vans were a familiar sight during the 1950s and 1960s, often parked in prominent places in town centres or in the grounds of large factories.

The compulsory free vaccination against smallpox introduced in the nineteenth century meant that this was another disease that had almost been eradicated. It was considered that the earlier a child was vaccinated the better, and the general advice was that it should be between 1 and 4 months, when there was less risk of the complications that could come later. The method used in the 1950s involved one scratch on either the arm or the leg, which was a vast improvement on the four distinctive marks that

> *'Whatever baby's state of health may be, don't let more than twenty-four hours go by without giving him his dose of fresh fruit juice.'*

scarred the arms of women born earlier. There was also immunisation available for diphtheria, a highly infectious and serious illness which could initially be mistaken for a really bad cold or swollen glands. Prompt hospital treatment in an isolation unit was essential to recovery but even so the patient might be left with the after effects of complications. There were other diseases which might require prompt hospital treatment but fortunately by the early 1950s new drugs as well as vaccines were available to help combat them.

Let Alan tell you his recollections of what happened to him, just before his fifth birthday:

In 1953 all my family were ill with the flu, except my Dad. I went down hill so very quickly the doctor was called out at night and he believed that the flu had become pneumonia. An ambulance was called and I was taken to Whips Cross Hospital, a converted workhouse they still use today. I was taken off the main ward and put into a side room with another boy. (This was usually a bad sign. I can only believe that my companion was also suffering from pneumonia. I have always wondered if his luck held.)

Only my Dad could visit, as the others were still ill at home. The doctor diagnosed Pulmonary Pneumonia. This, as you know, is where your lungs fill with liquid and the outcome is not very nice.

My Dad told me later that he asked the doctor if I would die; he replied 'I am not a miracle worker' but they should know in the next 48 hours. Well, here I have to be grateful to penicillin – in 1953 that's all they had. Fortunately I was lucky, the fever broke and I am still here today.

I was so weak my Dad had to carry me home when I was discharged. Just prior to going home my Dad gave me a teddy bear, which I still have today in my bedroom in his own special chair. And on returning home on the kitchen table was a band and troop toy soldiers of the Coldstream Guards. Funny to think they were all made of lead, nowadays they would certainly kill you! (Different times!)

Later, every fortnight or so, I had to go to a clinic for what was called Sun Ray treatment. Sitting on the side of a bed my back and front were warmed by a lamp giving off these rays. I sat there wearing a type of protective motorcycle goggles to protect my eyes from the light. My Mum was most careful that I always wore my vest to keep my body warm. I still do. Today (2012) I have just had my chest X-rayed at the hospital and there is a mark on one lung. The hospital always thinks I had TB, but fortunately I know better.

A mother of the 1950s onwards had much to be grateful for; the strides made in medical research had given her child the chance not only of a healthy life, but a long one too, so it was up to her to make sure that the child had all the injections it needed, not only in the first few months but also the boosters when they were needed. She must also bear in mind the advice in *You and Your Baby*: 'Whatever baby's state of health may be, don't let more than twenty-four hours go by without giving him his dose of fresh fruit juice. This contains vitamin C, which is an essential part of the daily diet. Should fruit juice disagree with baby, use an artificial source of vitamin C instead, that is tablets.' However much a mother did to ensure the health of her baby, there were still problems that could arise over which she had no control. Take what happened in Helen's family. Her story, while very sad, also throws light on an interesting piece of social history. Helen was born in December 1949 at the mother and babies hospital in Clapton, London. This maternity hospital had been opened in the late nineteenth century by the Salvation Army, originally to provide for the needs of unmarried mothers and the very poor, but later its doors were opened to any mother living in the neighbourhood. Although it was to become part of the NHS it retained its close association with the religious organisation:

The scandal of thalidomide left a generation severely disabled in a way that had never been seen before, and we hope and pray will not be witnessed again.

I was the eldest of three. My brother Paul who was two years younger than me, suffered from congenital heart disease. He was under Great Ormond Street and Whips Cross Hospital in Leytonstone. Being so young I have vague memories about this but because Mum had to take my brother back and forwards to hospital so often and was very busy with him, I didn't start school until I was nearly six. As my Mum and brother were well known, Mrs Edwards, the headmistress of the infants school which was right opposite where we lived, would send school work to Mum and she taught me to read and write. I could read by the age of four and still remember Mum standing me in front of a clock and teaching me the time. My brother who was a very clever little boy loved being shown what I was learning.

My sister was born in 1954. She was born at home, as they did in those days, but then she was rushed into hospital as Mum had rhesus negative blood, which meant my sister had to have her blood changed. As you can imagine Mum now had her hands very full – no washing machines or microwaves in those days.

Unfortunately Paul died in 1956 at the age of four. I was six and missed him dreadfully. I was put under Whips Cross Hospital as it was thought that I was having a nervous breakdown as a result of losing him. All my hair fell out and Mum and Dad had to rub this horrible stuff into my scalp – I often wonder what it was but it must have done me some good as my hair does go out of control if I don't keep it short. Later that year, Mum had another baby, Philip, but he lived only a couple of weeks.

I hope I don't sound depressing but this was how it was in those days. A lot of women had babies that died young or had health problems. Thank God those times have changed.

With the greater reliance upon the NHS came the public's increasing faith in the new wonder drugs that were being developed throughout the world. So it was that in

1958 thousands of women in Britain who experienced serious problems with morning sickness in the early stages of pregnancy, jumped at the chance of taking the pills that would alleviate the condition. It was only when it was discovered that there was a high incidence of birth defects in the babies whose mothers had taken these pills that they were withdrawn from use in 1961. The scandal of thalidomide left a generation severely disabled in a way that had never been seen before, and we hope and pray will not be witnessed again.

Another disease that came unexpectedly to the fore in the 1950s was leukaemia that affected both adults and children. Although it was a type of cancer that had long been known to medical science, it had not been talked about or actually named as far as the general public was concerned. It is believed now that in earlier times those who had it were likely to have died from other causes before the cancer had had time to develop fully. When it was noted that clusters of children in different parts of the country were diagnosed with this cancer, which was almost always fatal, there was widespread alarm and speculation as to the cause of this sudden breakdown in what had appeared until that time to be perfectly healthy blood cells. It was agonising for parents to watch as their once robust and lively children slowly declined, despite numerous blood transfusions and drug treatment.

The incidence of leukaemia in men who had worked at the Windscale nuclear power station seemed to point to the disease being in some way related to possible leaks from this new form of power. No one knew how much damaging radiation had already got into the atmosphere following the detonation of the atomic and hydrogen bombs at the end of the war or what would result from the experiments with nuclear explosions which continued throughout the 1950s in different parts of the world, Australia in particular. In addition, there were theories that those living under electricity pylons were also susceptible to both leukaemia and physical handicaps. Rumours and theories proliferated but they were little consolation to those who lost their innocent children or husbands and fathers or were left to bring up severely handicapped children.

'When the parents were informed that their child was 'handicapped', they were usually asked if they intended to keep it.

In the 1950s expectations were raised that the progress made in modern science would eventually rid us of diseases from the past, such as smallpox, TB, diphtheria, polio, measles, mumps and whooping cough; all would finally be eradicated thanks to the mass availability of vaccinations, inoculations and wonder drugs. It would seem that just when this was thought to be happening, newly discovered diseases have come along to take their place, while complacency on the part of some parents has allowed serious outbreaks of a number of the childhood ailments to flourish. Most 1950s mothers would have considered they had failed in their responsibility to their baby if they had neglected to visit either the doctor or their health clinic for baby's injections.

An expectant mother could make sure that throughout her pregnancy she did everything correctly but might still end up giving birth to a baby who was, as we have already discussed, malformed in some way. That would have been immediately discovered but it might have taken several days before the doctors broke the news that your beautiful little son or daughter was 'mongoloid'. That was the term used then for what we now know as a child suffering from Down's syndrome. When the parents were informed that their child was 'handicapped', they were usually asked if they intended to keep it. Previous generations had tended to hide such children away from the public gaze in special 'homes'. For a start it was assumed that their educational needs could not be met in ordinary schools and that their physical disabilities would place a great strain on family life. In 1956 a mother, on being told that she was ready to be discharged from the nursing home, was informed she could leave it with them to make the arrangements for her daughter to be taken straight to an institution. 'Go home and forget you ever had her,' were words that haunted her for years, even though she ignored all the advice she was given and insisted on keeping her baby with her. Like so much in the medical field, great advances have been made in the treatment and understanding of those suffering from both mental and physical problems, and along the way we have rid the language of some hurtful names and labels.

14

Training the Child: The Early Years

*I*f one followed the advice in the books then it was up to every mother to 'train' her child. This training was to start almost from the moment of birth and, it seemed, revolved around two things; the first was getting the baby in the habit of doing what mother wanted at all times and the second seemed to be the obsession with 'potty training'. We have already seen that some of the advice had the baby only a few days after birth being held over a receptacle in an effort to accustom it to urinate and evacuate as a reflex action. Other books took a more relaxed attitude until the child was at the toddling stage but then, if we are to follow the suggested timetable in the *Sunday Express Baby Book*, it seemed to dominate the daily routine:

6.45 am.	Take him up to urinate (the time will depend upon when he

	usually wakes.) Put him back into a dry bed.
7.00 am.	Rises, urinates, gets light sponge bath. Breakfast …
7.30 am.	On toilet for bowel movement …
9.00 am.	Urinates before going out to play in pen or garden.
11.00 am.	Brought in to toilet …
12. noon.	On toilet …
2 – 3.00 pm.	Wakes from nap. Placed on toilet …
5.00 pm.	Urinates …
5.30 – 6.00 pm.	Supper … urinates.
7.00 pm.	On toilet again.
10.00 pm.	Take up, place on toilet to urinate. Afterwards given dry clothes and bed if necessary.

The conscientious mother who tried to follow this regime to the letter could end up totally frustrated when the child's performances did not match the text-book. Such was the case of little Simon whose mother asked one of the magazines how she could have her 2-year-old dry in time for the arrival of a new baby. The mother reported that Simon had started using his pot very well from about 3 weeks old (!) but when he was a year he started refusing it and had not used it since. The health visitor giving advice wrote:

'It is a common mistake to think because a baby uses the pot when he is put on it that he is trained. Training means teaching a child to control what he is doing, whereas a young baby is quite incapable of controlling his motions consciously. A child isn't really trained until he knows what the pot is for and decides that he will use it in preference to soiling himself.'

The advice to Simon's mother was that she should forget all about it for a couple of weeks and then, in the most relaxed manner, try again producing the pot two or three times rather than the hourly trips she had been making with him. It would seem that Simon's mother might have read the regime suggested above. However, our health visitor sensibly pointed out that hourly trips were not helping the child's bladder get used to holding larger quantities. The whole toilet training issue became just that – an issue, instead of a natural part of growing up. In the 1950s those mothers, who sometimes despaired of ever getting their child dry, were often comforted by the statement: 'no child of five ever starts school wearing nappies!' It may be one of those apocryphal stories but it has been said that the widespread use of disposable nappy pants has led to some twenty-first-century children doing just that.

One understands that the foster mother had to be careful not to get emotionally involved with the baby, so she looked after his physical needs well but he had not received any love.

One of the earliest words a mother taught her baby was to say 'thank you' - usually shortened to 'ta'.

So let us avoid the use of the word training and concentrate instead on learning. Every mother wants the best for her child and hopes that she will teach her baby to grow up to be a healthy and happy human being, one who will enjoy his life, take advantage of the opportunities that come his way and do well in his chosen work, but above all that he will remain the loving and lovable person he was as a child. The mother achieves much of this not by any deliberate teaching plan but rather by the example of her own behaviour. Of course father has a great part in all this too but certainly in the 1950s, as we have noted, his role was not quite so important in the very early years as was mother's.

'I did read some books and magazine articles and I listened to the nurses at the clinic and the health visitor but mainly I used my commonsense and instinct.' These words occurred over and over from the women who helped with this work. Somehow, once the new mother had overcome her fears about caring for the baby and, as the weeks passed, she became more used to handling it, so it seemed that instinct did indeed take over. It was probably easier for those who had younger brothers and sisters they had helped to look after, or if they were the youngest in the family then they may have been involved in caring for nephews and nieces. In being part of a large family group a girl learned much about childcare, often without realising it, just as she picked up the rudiments of cooking and housework through helping her mother.

The specialist books stressed how important it was that the mother train her infant to follow the daily routine they prescribed: to take his cod liver oil without spitting it out; to perform (like Pavlov's dogs) when he felt the cold rim of a chamber pot against his bottom; not to expect every cry to be answered and so on. But it fell to mother actually to teach her child to understand the world into which he had been born. And the first thing mother, and father too, taught

their child was the security that comes with uncom-
promising love. A baby learnt this much sooner than
many thought possible, as was proved in the case of
baby D. His birth mother was unable to keep him so
he was taken from hospital to a foster mother for
six weeks prior to his adoption. When he was taken
home by his new parents, a couple who for years
had been unable to have a child, they were thrilled
with the beautiful, well-nourished baby who slept
through the night, took his bottle as he should and
rarely cried. He was the textbook good baby – except
for one thing: he did not respond to the cuddles that
his new mother and father longed to give him. One
understands that the foster mother had to be careful
not to get emotionally involved with the baby, so she
looked after his physical needs well but he had not
received any love. It took the new parents time and
patience to teach their little son that he was loved.
And the love and security he experienced as a child in
turn gave him the ability to give love to others, leading him into a happy and secure marriage and family
life with children and grandchildren.

In preparing her little one to take his place in the
world, the mother taught her child to obey not just her
rules of behaviour but those more generally accepted in
the community as a whole.
For example, although
it might be fun to blow
bubbles in his milk,
this was not to be rec-
ommended more than
once or twice. The time for
blowing bubbles was in the bath
or out in the garden with a bubble pipe and a bowl
of soapy water. Similarly, the natural reflex to spit

*The toddler in his playpen
would laugh and clap his hands as
he watched mother pirouette round
the room as she dusted.*

out anything with an unpleasant taste had to be controlled, while it was explained to the child that the very act of spitting was unacceptable behaviour, whether it was spitting out food or, worse, spitting in the face of another child, especially as such expectoration could cause illnesses. In spite of notices that appeared on trains and public transport vehicles threatening fines for anyone caught spitting, there were still those, mainly men, who cleared their throats into the gutter or else straight on to the pavement as they walked through towns.

One of the earliest words a mother taught her baby was to say 'thank you' – usually shortened to 'ta'. As she went about her work, if the baby offered her one of his toys she would thank him and often used the word for him when she gave him anything. Gradually, it became a habit and then 'please' was added. Baby would hold out his hands for something and mother would say, 'what do you say?' and wait for the child's own version of the words for please and thank you. As the child grew older it was important that he should always be polite when offered something by other people, remembering his 'Ps & Qs', as it was called at that time. Along with thanks, the child learnt not to snatch items but to wait until they were offered. A more difficult lesson in social behaviour, because it often arose in situations that gave mothers acute embarrassment, was how to react to the small child who bit another child. The baby advice books are quiet on this subject. Grandmothers advised either that the offending child should receive a short sharp slap on the hand or leg or that the mother should sink her teeth into the same part of the anatomy as the child had just done, 'so he knows what it feels like'. Like everything else, it depended on the temperament of both mother and child how the matter should be dealt with. This brings us to the burning question of 'To smack or not to smack?'

Most parents in the 1950s would have grown up accustomed to punishments that varied from the 'clip round the ear' through to smacking on arms, legs and bottoms, to quite hard beatings with the back of a hairbrush or a thin cane. No doubt most of those who had suffered at least one of these forms of punishments would have vowed at sometime that they would never inflict such behaviour on their own children. However, that was sometimes easier said than done and while a parent was well aware that it was demeaning to lose one's temper with a small child, there were times when a toddler's behaviour had mother almost at screaming point. (What had mother done or neglected to do to have reached this state, Miss Liddiard would have asked!) The sensible thing was to remove the child to a safe place such as his playpen or bedroom until the parent had calmed down, rather than administering a smart slap on the hand and a firm 'NO!' It was all very well trying to explain gently to the child that whatever he was doing was wrong or unacceptable but that did not always work and putting the child into his room alone could also backfire, as one mother found out when she, having regained her composure, entered the child's room to find that her daughter had scribbled all over the beautifully decorated walls with black and dark brown crayons. Experts would have advised her to harness her daughter's artistic talent, but she was more concerned that she was then faced with the additional chore of cleaning the walls. Mothers are many things but they are not all blessed, all the time, with the patience of the proverbial saint.

Almost from birth mother started teaching her baby to appreciate rhythm and sound. When she held the child against her shoulder to bring up wind, her hand would unconsciously adopt a steady beat against the infant's back or bottom. When he cried she would gently jiggle him up and down and more often as not would quietly sing to him. What she sang did not really matter, though strangely, years later a child might identify a song he had heard dating from that time. Throughout the ages mothers have routinely sung lullabies to their babies, the somewhat monotonous rhythm usually sending them off to sleep. In some cases one particular song became so associated with going to sleep that the child always asked for it. Children love to sing too. During the 1950s, young children probably grew accustomed to hearing music in the background as their mothers listened to radio programmes such as *Housewives' Choice* as they went about their work. Constant repetition of the songs played soon had the child recognising both the tune and the words. Other mothers would put records on the radiogram, songs perhaps from the latest show or favourite classical pieces, all of which encouraged the child to react to the music. The toddler in his playpen would laugh and clap his hands as he watched mother pirouette round the room as she dusted. All the time he was learning.

While he was still very tiny, he was hearing numbers as mother carried him up to bed. Starting at the bottom of the flight, she would carefully intone the number for each stair – usually twelve or thirteen – and when she carried him down in the morning she would count them again. This was not deliberate teaching as such, but mother talking and encouraging her child in the use of language. In the same way, as the child grew, so mother would name parts of his body, longing to hear him repeat the words 'nose', 'teeth', 'chin' and 'tummy'. It was all one big game. Surprisingly, a baby had to be taught to play. Would he, if left to himself, learn to play? Given, for example, a pile of toy bricks, a young child would explore their shape and feel – and taste, because everything went into a baby's mouth! But would he, without the intervention of his parents, start to build the bricks into a tower and then have the fun of knocking it over and starting all over again? Would a child left to himself get the sensory pleasure of walking through dry leaves in autumn or, wearing his waterproof boots, wade into a puddle both to make a splash and disturb the coloured film on its surface? It was up to mother during the course of each day, to introduce her child to new experiences and to help develop the child's imagination. And because most 1950s mothers were at home all day with their under fives, they did just that. Reception class teachers soon spotted the very quiet, amenable child who did exactly as she was told; for it was usually a little girl, who had been brought up to a rigid timetable, spending long periods in a room on her own with little or no contact with other children. Like the young labrador that was offered to the police for training, it was discovered that he had not learned as a puppy how to play and consequently he was rejected as unsuitable for police work. By the time he was again rehomed, it was too late to teach him to do the simple fetching of sticks and balls. Fortunately, this was not the

It was up to mother during the course of each day to introduce her child to new experiences and to help develop the child's imagination.

case with schoolchildren but they had lost five valuable years of experiencing fun and imaginative play.

Parents introduced their babies both to play and the development of their imagination by providing them with suitable playthings. Like every other manufacturer in the 1950s toy makers had yet to get back to pre-war production. It would take time before there were sufficient supplies of metal available for the production of pedal cars and dolls' prams, which were often the first big toys for a small child. For this reason, many early 1950s toddlers received a much-loved and cherished but outgrown second-hand item. Not that they really cared. However, things were different once the toy makers began manufacturing in plastic. This not only brought the price down for large items like pedal cars and rocking horses, it also introduced many small items, that unlike metal toys, were much safer for a small child to play with. Even the humble bucket and spade were produced in moulded plastic and this meant that the bucket could become a bath toy instead of being used only at the seaside.

Baby's first toy was likely to be a teddy bear or a soft toy animal. Our baby experts always advised that soft toys should be washable, for obvious reasons. This was where the home knitter came to the fore. Close to Christmas, grandma, granny or nana, as well as any doting aunts, could put aside the Fair Isle jumper or double-knit cardigan and, scouring the pages of their women's magazines, they found toys to make that would serve as ideal presents. For example, in October 1952 *Stitchcraft* provided instructions for making a knitted doll, complete with clothes that included shoes and socks, and a delightful cuddly puppy and kitten. The following year they presented Woofy, a most appealing puppy with floppy ears and another knitted doll called Topsy. In the politically correct years that have followed neither Topsy nor the golliwog have been allowed to appear, but there she was in 1953 with a complete wardrobe and no doubt became greatly loved by all who were given her. The December 1958 issue contained an unusual snowman but also, utilising a new brand of wool called Fuzzy-Wuzzy which resembled angora, there were instructions for a miniature poodle and a cuddly rabbit. In the following January issue, the magazine editors must have taken note of the small dolls, about 6in or so in height, which came in pairs, providing little girls with a family of twins. Many magazines then and since have provided outfits for these dolls; on this occasion the girl doll had skirt, cardigan and bonnet while her brother had trousers, a jumper knitted with a cable pattern and a cap with a bobble on the top.

On the subject of dolls, it had been noted that little boys liked playing with them too, if they were given the opportunity.

It seems likely that Christmas 1958 had seen record sales of dolls' prams and little cots, both of which would need the lovely knitted blanket, directions for which appeared in that same January issue of the magazine. On the subject of dolls, it had been noted that little boys liked playing with them too, if they were given the opportunity. Some parents, fathers in the main, were not particularly happy about their young son showing an interest in a doll. However, it was not quite so bad if

Instinctively most mothers started singing or saying nursery rhymes to their babies.

it was a boy doll, dressed as a boy and as long as the child did not take it out with him in public! In the years that followed the American toy manufacturers were to exploit the masculine interest with the introduction of Ken and Action Man. Similarly, male interests were catered for with the introduction of the very wide range of Dinky cars, which again helped develop the child's imagination as he acted out his own scenarios with his cars and lorries.

Like so much else, the rationing of paper had affected the production of books in the immediate post-war period. When production increased books were relatively expensive, so parents had to think carefully before allowing their little ones to handle the precious books from their own childhood. This was one reason why reading to one's child became so widespread. It was also a very intimate time for parents to sit with a child cuddled up close to look at the pictures as they either read from the actual text or made up a story suggested by the pictures. The child learned so much from these sessions. To start with they had to sit still in order to see the pictures; they needed to be quiet to hear what was being read or told; they were able to stop the reader and ask questions – and receive an answer; they acquired language, absorbing it like a sponge; and their imaginations were fired by what they heard. Instinctively most mothers started singing or saying nursery rhymes to their babies. Quite a tiny baby would respond to the toe-tickling: *This Little Piggy went to Market* or *Round and Round the Garden* on the palm of the hand. One just had to be careful, according to Miss Liddiard, not to stimulate the child with too much tickling. Giggles always followed a session of *This is the Way the Gentlemen Ride*, the adult probably tiring of it long before the child did! From this, one progressed to repeating the nursery rhymes that one had heard in one's own childhood; almost inevitably one would have unconsciously started with *Hush-a-bye Baby* as one rocked a sleepy baby. An example of absorption of language was shown by Mrs L's A. As she wrote in her *Sunday Express Baby Book*:

> He speaks well at twenty months. He knows the last words of the lines of fifteen nursery rhymes. Also he recited the whole of Georgie Porgy without being prompted, although he was never taught it.

From the constant repetition of rhymes, parents moved on to the well-loved stories such as the *Three Little Pigs*; these gave them both the added fun of chorusing 'I'll huff and I'll puff …' the 'Fee, Fi, Fo, Fum …' of *Jack and the Beanstalk*. Without realising it, parents were passing on their cultural heritage and reliving memories of their own childhood. It was a strange moment when, while reading one of the fairy stories that one had loved as a child, one stopped to consider the horror contained in some of them. Should one protect one's little cherub from being upset that the wolf had eaten grandma? Not a bit of it – the child accepted it and if he had heard the story before would not allow any changes or deviation from the original. The squeamish parent would have welcomed some of the very bland little books that appeared in the 1950s which depicted happy families and good boys and girls, but children approaching thier fifth birthday had already become

Should one protect one's little cherub from being upset that the wolf had eaten grandma?

more realistic and wanted more adventurous stories – that was why Enid Blyton was so popular.

If, as the books told us, it was the duty of the mother to train her child, then if she had provided stimulating playthings; had introduced her little one to the world of music and language; had inspired his imagination and developed creativity with paint, crayon or plasticine – then she was on the way to having fulfilled that duty. Further, if she had produced a happy, confident child who was amenable to discipline when necessary, polite, well behaved and a joy to be with, then she was to be warmly congratulated – it certainly was not easy!

15

Endings and Beginnings

For almost five years our 1950s mother has been the centre of her baby's world. After the nine months he was part of her body, she experienced the pain and joy of bringing him into the world. The close bond between mother and child was reinforced in those daily periods when she held him close and suckled him. For the first few months he was entirely dependent on her to supply his every need. In the next two or three years his dependency grew into his love and admiration for this wonderful mother, who not only knew all there was to know in the big wide world outside his home but was also able to do so many different things. He followed her around the house perpetually asking questions, imitating what she did, playing at being mummy, helping to cook by using the left-over pastry to make biscuits, or in the garden playing make believe games of keeping house and making mud pies for dinner. He might have a small circle of friends to play with occasionally but on the whole, since he spent practically all his time with his mother, she was his playmate too. The 1950s books on bringing up baby might prescribe a routine for the first year of baby's life, but after that, apart from good advice on keeping up with regular trips to the clinic for inoculations, dental checks, eye and hearing tests, it was up to the individual mother how she organised her time with her toddler.

There could not be any hard and fast rules apart from the need for her to do the daily household chores, the shopping and produce possibly three home-cooked meals a day for her husband, herself and the children. It was taken for granted that the great majority of 1950s mothers did not go out to work, so all the children's early development depended on them. The 1950s housewife was encouraged to be house-proud. Once she had a house that was just for her family and not a couple of rooms in a shared house, then there was tremendous incentive for her home to be kept as immaculately as possible. Lacking many of the machines we now consider essential, mothers on the whole managed to complete most of the domestic work during the morning. After lunch and a sit-down for a story on the radio programme, *Listen with Mother*, the afternoons were free for taking the child or children out for a walk that may have included a trip to the shops. If the weather was bad then it was during the afternoon that mother would introduce activities like

Babyhood had ended and a new chapter in the child's life began with going to school.

colouring with crayons, creating figures and shapes with plasticine, cutting out pictures and sticking them into scrapbooks, sewing card pictures – such a number of things to show daddy when he came home from work. And when it was time for bed, perhaps daddy would read him a story – or possibly show great astonishment when his son or daughter produced a favourite book and proceeded to 'read' every word accurately.

What was happening was that instinctively, the 1950s mother was preparing herself for that day, fast approaching as her child entered his fifth year, when she would be supplanted by another woman who would become the centre of her child's world, unconsciously taking her child's affection and a woman who would frequently be quoted to his mother in those dreaded words, 'but Miss says …' Babyhood had ended and a new chapter in the child's life began with going to school. Di remembered:

> My first day at school must have been early in September 1950. I distinctly recall being out in the back garden in the new school dress my mummy had made for me, blue check Vyella with a trim of braid at the waist and neck featuring Mickey Mouse. I was so excited I was calling over the fence to tell a neighbour all about it very early in the day before the short walk to the place itself. And the actuality did not disappoint. Miss Ford was our teacher, a kind and happy Christian soul, (even in those days my parents chose to send me to a strong church school) who always wore a smock, I suppose to protect herself from five year old fingers. There must have been 30 to 40 children in the class, and some of them were still classmates at the end of sixth form at the local grammar school. The room seemed huge and

I can remember the windows being very high up, all you could see was sky and the top of a tall horse chestnut tree in the playground. Great importance was attached to reading and I quickly became very fond of *Old Lob*, *Dan the dog* and *Dobbin the horse*. The alphabet, showing upper and lower case letters, was displayed on the wall, and there were 'corners' for the nature table, the story books and figures we made to recount the scripture stories we heard. There was an enormous coke stove, which hissed and sang, and the caretaker used to come in and make it up during the course of the day with much clanging and puffing. He also placed the milk crate close up to it in the winter so that the milk was warm by playtime. There was a tall guard surrounding the stove and this was frequently hung with wet socks and other things.

Being not that long after the war there was still rationing, especially sweets. Miss Ford had a friend in Hungary who sent her a copy of the Gingerbread House made of cake and sweets and I clearly remember sitting on the floor round her feet listening to the story of *Hansel and Gretel* and then being given something delicious [to eat]. I also remember sitting on the floor when we had a student teacher blessed with the name of Miss Pip. She had a closed box on her knee from which came curious rustlings. After a tantalising build up she eventually produced a live hedgehog! Think of all those health and safety issues involved nowadays.

In that first year Miss Ford produced work cards covering Hundreds, Tens and Units not to mention Shillings and Pence. I can see them still, handwritten in black ink on pink card. She must have worked very hard at helping us to master what were quite difficult basics, not to mention a wind-round 'cinema' housed in an orange box featuring *Old Lob* himself. There were PE lessons in the playground and the advent of a rope net stretched over a frame which we had to climb. The toilets were in the playground away from the school building and gosh they smelt strong. Miss Ford had a very comfortable lap if you were upset and she was the best puller-out of milk teeth the world has ever known.

We have noted earlier that the decade of the 1950s was the pivot between the old order and the new, and this shows very clearly in attitudes towards education. The process had been started with the 1944 Act which revolutionised secondary education by making places at grammar schools free to all those who passed the eleven-plus examination, thus opening the way to a university education to bright children from homes with limited incomes. The newly created secondary modern schools added more practical subjects to the curriculum, like office skills, woodwork and technical drawing, in an attempt to educate the workforce needed for an expanding industrial economy. However, by the middle of the 1950s, the growing socialistic ideas of equality of opportunity for all led to the creation of the first comprehensive schools, their exponents believing that observations of the systems used in both the United States and the USSR seemed to point the way this country should go as well, to

Apart from the classrooms there was also a large hall that could be used for morning assembly as well as activities like PE, drama, music and dancing.

achieve well-rounded students. But while arguments and ideals clashed over what was best for the older age groups, consideration had to be given to those just starting out.

Di, like a number of other '1950s children', spent her first years at a school that was probably built in late Victorian or Edwardian times. Living as she did on the outskirts of London, her school building had escaped the bombing. Like a vast number of Victorian schools, it had been erected under the auspices of the Church of England and that was why it had the same red-brick Gothic style with high pointed windows so reminiscent of much of the late nineteenth-century church architecture. The schools, originally built to take children of all ages, had separate entrances for boys, girls and infants, and a concrete-paved playground for each, with a possible plane tree or two on the perimeter. Anyone who came into one of the London stations by train in the 1950s will recall just how depressing some of these schools looked. Inside the teachers did their best to enliven the cream- or green-painted walls by hanging bright pictures and posters. The classrooms had tall ceilings that made them seem big, as indeed they needed to be, as they catered for up to forty children. The infants sat at low wooden tables on wooden chairs suitable for small bottoms. The tables could be arranged round three sides of the room, the children sitting behind the tables, quite close to their neighbours but with elbow room, and all of them able to see the teacher, and more importantly, she could see them. In those days when chalk and talk was still fashionable, the Miss Fords of this world would have had a blackboard perched on a large easel at the front of the class. This was used not only to demonstrate the beginnings of writing and arithmetic, but was also used as a support when needed for the large shiny cloth-backed maps and large sheets for reading practice or singing. The easel was situated close to the teacher's desk. In the early 1950s, that heavy wooden desk, of a design that would have been at home in a Victorian counting house, would have been built up on a small platform so that when she sat in her seat the teacher had a commanding view of the whole scene ahead of her.

The large numbers of council estates that were built throughout the country to alleviate the acute housing shortage following the war meant that most of the homes were occupied by young families, so it was essential that, along with shops, a primary school should be included in the planning. So it was out with Victoriana and in with modern, one-storey, concrete and glass buildings, with an unfortunate use of asbestos in their construction. Apart from the classrooms there was also a large hall that could be used for morning assembly as well as activities like PE, drama, music and dancing. Some readers may instantly recall those wonderful radio *Music and Movement* programmes where the cheerfully brisk lady urged her listeners, clad in vest, knickers or shorts, to spread out round the room and pretend to be trees by stretching up tall or to crouch down as small as little rabbits before hopping round the hall.

In 1958, Colleen went to the school on her estate:

I was waiting with my Mum, firmly holding her hand at times for reassurance outside the school in a queue of other Mums and children, all waiting for the school gates to open for our first frightening day in a strange place. I can remember a boy in front of us started crying and desperately wanting to drag his Mum home. I wanted to cry with him but decided I was too big a girl to do a baby thing! My Mum explained that he cried because he was scared. Eventually someone from the school came out and the boy and his Mother were taken into school leaving the rest of us waiting. I remember thinking that he'd be in his pyjamas now and taken to bed but would still have to stay in school ... Once we were allowed in the grounds I know we had our names called out and we went into <u>that</u> line. An adult appeared in front of our queues and we were told to follow this person into the new classroom. As we went in, the parents left. By this time I was happy for Mum to go as I had other things occupying me. My first teacher took us inside and I believe we chose where to sit, she was Miss Denby and I immediately liked her, she was kind. I remember too that I had a little vanity case with me to carry my things. We sat at rows of tables linked in a line. I sat with my back to the door, surrounded by children I didn't know. We looked at each other and warily smiled. On the classroom walls was the alphabet with each letter having a picture. When it was quiet I used to go over the alphabet a lot, reading the walls. I also befriended a girl because she had tiny, delicate hands and I held her hand all through break time.

It is a fact that most people can remember the name of their first teacher, usually with great affection.

It seems that regardless of the year or the place in the country, most children's experience of their first days in the infants' class was very similar. Outstanding was the fact that practically every one of the '1950s children' remembered their teacher's name and bore testimony to her kindness. We should doubtless remark on the patience of these dedicated women. The other thing that did not seem to change was the fear of using the school lavatories. In Colleen's case:

> I was scared of going to the toilet so I used to force myself not to go. I'd spend ages in there 'not' going as I'd decided I'd wait till I got home, however many hours away that was!

Countless other children must have decided on the same policy and during those first few weeks, as they settled in, Miss found herself having to provide spare knickers and shorts for those who had 'little accidents', and then the school caretaker would appear with a dustpan full of sawdust to scatter on the floor.

It is a fact that most people can remember the name of their first teacher, usually with great affection. Most of the 1950s children who started school in the first half of the decade were taught by ladies who had, it seemed, been at the school forever. They had certainly had to put up with a great deal during their careers, especially during the 1940s. Some had been evacuated with their classes to different parts of the country, finding themselves sharing premises with other schools and in some cases acting as surrogate mothers to those children who were unaccompanied. Most of these women had trained long ago and were happily carrying on with the tried-and-tested teaching methods of the time. Very different was young Mrs G, who qualified as an infants teacher in 1953. Her training had been based on all the very latest in educational thinking. Here was not the plump, cosy, white-haired lady who smelled of lavender and wore home-knitted cardigans, but a very young, modern Miss. When she took up her first post in September 1953 she found herself with a class of forty-three. In those days 5-year-olds were admitted to school at the beginning of each of the three terms that began in January, April and September. Because

'The children settled in well, although some had to be dragged in crying, but this was often while the parent was there, and stopped once the parent had gone'.

the school was on one of the new estates, it so happened that all the children who formed her class had been 5 within three months of each other and so they had all started their school life the previous term following the Easter holiday. Thus they were, to use her words, 'already broken in', which was probably just as well for her, as in those days there was no classroom assistant to help her through the trauma of the first day. Never mind the children, often the first thing the teacher had to do when welcoming the new intake was to try to persuade the mother that her child would be quite all right once she had left:

> The children settled in well, although some had to be dragged in crying, but this was often while the parent was there, and stopped once the parent had gone. In one case I had to go and comfort the mother once I'd settled the child!

Mrs G also recounted a similar episode that throws up a piece of 1950s social history. She was teaching in a part of the country where there were still fully operational United States airbases. The US Government ensured

that each base provided schools for the children of
their personnel but followed the system in the States,
which meant the children did not start there until they
were 6. Since many of the married servicemen lived in
the local community; by law their 5-year-olds had to
attend school. 'We had an American Dad in once with
his new reception daughter and, at playtime, he was
still there saying, "Can I go now, honey?".'

Mrs G also remarked on the acute overcrowding
in schools during the 1950s. During her time she and
her class spent a whole academic year in each of the
following: the infant dining room, the junior dining
room, the infant hall and the infant staff room. So
overcrowded did this infant/junior school become
that one year a class was housed in the partially built
secondary school nearby. Apart from the disruptions
caused by the rooms being used for other purposes, it
was very difficult for the teacher to display work on
the walls or on tables.

As with so many other aspects of life in the 1950s,
teachers had to adapt to the different situations in
which they found themselves. A lack of ready-made
teaching aids and equipment meant that they had to
make their own, such as writing individual number
sheets for each child and
even sewing sheets to
form exercise books
to compensate for
the paper short-
age left by the war.
Apart from having
to deal with cultural
differences raised by the
American children, some schools found themselves
having to deal with numbers of children who spoke

With a large class, it was sometimes difficult to cater for the needs of a 5 year old who was aalready more advanced than his classmates.

little or no English. These included the offspring of those members of the Polish army who, having fought alongside the British during the war, had chosen to remain in this country rather than returning home when peace was declared. Other children came from families where one parent spoke a foreign language so often they came to school speaking a mixture of languages. Towards the end of the 1950s, in many areas classes were filled with children of African origin from the Caribbean who did speak English, as well as those from India who did not. Somehow the teacher had to set to and teach every child how to read and write as well as making sure that every child could actually understand what was being said to him.

A number of the '1950s children' reported that they could read and write by the time they started school. On the whole these tended to be girls. In most cases they had been taught, though none could recall the actual process, by older sisters. Where there was a considerable age gap, such as the eight and eleven years that existed between Mary and her sisters, it was likely that the older girls had started by reading stories to their baby sister and from that had progressed to actual teaching. In other cases, a very keen 6-year-old like Helen was anxious to pass on her newly acquired skills to a younger sibling. There were mothers, too, who took the opportunity to amuse their children by showing them how to make letters and numbers, perhaps using a toy blackboard and easel, or a slate with coloured chalks. There were other mothers who, realising that their child was anxious to learn, made a conscious effort to teach them. In some cases the teaching profession frowned upon moves such as the *Teach Your Baby to Read* kits that came from the United States and enjoyed some popularity in the late 1950s and 1960s. With a large class, it was sometimes difficult to cater for the needs of a 5-year-old who was already more advanced than his classmates. The child who could already read and write fluently could either become bored and a nuisance or retired into a world of his own. However, Mrs G's experience was that very few of her 1950s pupils could write their names when they first came into school or, if they did, they used capital letters. There were some who could recognise their own names when it was written, which meant they were quickly able to find their own named clothes peg in the cloakroom area.

Mrs G did make the interesting comment, though, that compared with the infants she taught in later years, the language skills of little ones in the 1950s was better. The children were more articulate. However, she had noted that once TV had taken hold and the computer age had dawned, many children in the reception class had to be taught how to talk in sentences. If questioned, she would no doubt have said that the 1950s infant was better too at listening. The young child grew up in a home where he listened to what his mother was saying to him; he listened with her to programmes on the radio that gave him both speech and music; he listened as she sang to him, told him stories or simply just chatted. His world was dominated by sound and he had learned very early on that listening also involved sitting down and being quiet. The 1950s child was expected to remain

The 1950s child was expected to remain silent when his parents had visitors and certainly not butt in on adult conversation.

silent when his parents had visitors and certainly not butt in on adult conversation. It was as he or she sat quietly on the floor with a picture book or a toy that the child learned a great deal about adults and picked up snippets of information that could be stored away to reintroduce at a later date, usually at a most embarrassing moment.

On that subject, all parents of all children, including those of the 1950s, had to be prepared to have personal information about the family disclosed, not just to the teacher but to the whole class too, and so to the parents of all the children in the class. In the *Mother* magazine of January 1951 there is an article entitled 'Seen from the Classroom', written by an infants teacher to reassure mothers about their child starting school. Along with all the sensible remarks, the writer R.W.G. Graves makes an amusing observation that at the same time throws in an aside on the shortages still existing in 1951:

> Often he blossoms forth in less than an hour and then, dear mother, you really do have something to worry about! Throwing all caution to the winds and showing a remarkable absence of reticence, he launches into a detailed account of himself, progressing by stages to a history of every member of the family. It is useless to try to stop him. If there are skeletons in the family cupboard, then he is determined to give them an airing. If mother has certain views on Mrs Brown next door then it is his pleasure to recount them. If his teacher would like some little extras then little Johnny knows just where mother gets them and is fully prepared to pass on this helpful information to his new friend.

Unlike today where children are often taught in groups within a class, teaching where there was just the teacher had by necessity to be for the whole class. Mrs G taught reading using the 'look and say' method and 'whole word' recognition using structured reading schemes such as Happy Venture and Ladybird books. The old-fashioned phonic system that mother had learned was jettisoned in favour of the repetitious *Jane and Peter* and *Janet and John* books. As for number work, Mrs G reported that a number of new schemes were invented, designed and produced during the 1950s. Her head teacher chose to adopt the Cuisenaire scheme throughout the school and all the teachers were sent on courses at various times to learn how to operate it. Mrs G said they were supposed to use it all the time, which suggests that perhaps they did not! Mention Cuisenaire to today's young teachers and you are liable to be met with a blank stare, which is perhaps better than the 1950s domestic science teacher who wondered if the system had anything to do with cookery. Briefly, Cuisenaire was a Belgian schoolmaster who, during the 1930s, developed a system of using coloured rods as a way of making arithmetic fun. His book, published in 1952, had gained support worldwide and soon, as Mrs G reported, the method was adopted in most primary schools throughout the country. Each number between one and ten was given a wooden block or rod of increasing size and a different colour; thus 1cm was white; 2 red; 3 light green; 4 lavender; 5 yellow; 6 dark green; 7 black; 8 brown; 9 blue; and 10 orange. These colourful rods made delightful

For those children who could not return home or were entitled to a free meal, a hot dinner was provided at the school.

patterns and no doubt the children who used them understood what they were doing. However, to someone of a previous generation who had learned tables by rote and excelled at mental arithmetic, the response of 'lavender' from the small child who was asked what 2 + 2 made, was somewhat puzzling.

The teacher whose article appeared in the magazine warned mothers that for the first few days their children might return home hungry if they stayed to have school dinner. This, she assures mothers, was not because there was insufficient to eat, rather that the child would be far too interested in other things to bother about eating. It may be that this was the first time the child had had a communal meal outside his home and 'the novelty of it all is a bit too much; the remarkable sight of so many juvenile trenchermen in vigorous action is a sight not to be missed!' Mrs G would not have agreed with her since her experience was somewhat different. She pointed out that in the 1950s, infant and junior schools had a long break of two hours between morning and afternoon sessions. Since the school was part of the estate, it was quite possible for children to go home to eat, as mother would more than likely have cooked a meal for father who came home from work, to eat his lunch. For those children who could not return home or were entitled to a free meal, a hot dinner was provided at the school. In Mrs G's school there were insufficient numbers requiring them to warrant the meals being cooked on the premises, so theirs were delivered instead from a central kitchen. In young Miss' eyes these were unappetising and when she was not required to supervise those having dinner, she would, she confessed, visit the local fish and chip shop whenever it was open – a practice that would not be approved of today!

The *Mother* magazine article about starting school paints a delightful picture of all the exciting things that were available in the 1951 classroom:

> Some coloured beads, a jig-saw puzzle, a few pieces of pretty paper and a pair of blunt scissors and he's busy. Maybe he will have a ladder to climb or a wooden engine to push around ... the playground beckons after lunch with the exciting prospect of playing cowboys with unlimited Indians ... and as he walks through the door at the end of the day his parting shot may be, 'I may come to see you again soon!' His way of saying that school is not such a bad place after all.

During the 1950s the words 'free expression' were often bandied about in educational circles, leading to what then became known as a child-centred system. On their first day in one infants school, the teacher told the children that after playtime in the afternoon, they would be able to choose to do whatever they liked. One little boy took this statement at face value, telling his mother when he arrived home minus his outdoor clothes before she had time to set out to meet him at the school gate, that his choice was to go home!

One of the many exciting things about starting school was the discovery of new friends. For the child his world was suddenly expanded beyond that of his immediate and extended family and his local neighbourhood; he now came into contact with children who, while they were the same age, might come from a very different background or culture. Little girls very quickly found themselves a 'best friend' with whom to spend as much time as possible, a soul mate to fall-out with frequently, yet one to return to and retain right through schooldays and often well beyond. Both Di and Colleen testified to such friendships. Boys seemed to prefer to have a wider set of friends, to be part of a little gang in the school playground and after school, possibly in the road outside their home if it was safe to play there. The quieter, more reserved boys would somehow gravitate towards each other to play and were likely to exchange visits to each other's home to play there. Mothers had to learn not to interfere with their child's choice of friends. They might not be to their taste or not considered suitable company for their little darling, but it was better to be kind and friendly and keep one's fingers crossed that the child would discover for himself that he and his new friend had little in common. Voicing one's disapproval of one's offspring's choice of friend had the same effect on a 5-year-old as it would have some years later on a teenage daughter; it would only make the friend seem more attractive.

There were, however, some little friends that your child would bring home from school that you really could not entertain. In fact, you had to take drastic steps to eliminate them. It was possible that you had not noticed that your child had started scratch-

It was possible that you had not noticed that your child had started scratching his head.

ing his head. If you had, you may have put it down to tiredness, because your mother had always said that head scratching was a sure sign you should be in your bed. So if the tell-tale sign had been ignored, you now had to face the ignominy of receiving the

official letter which related that when the clinic nurse
had visited the school for one of her spot inspections,
your child had been found to have – NITS! The nit
nurse, aka Nitty Nora in some areas, was feared by
every schoolchild who knew what was in store for
them if they were found to have the dreaded eggs
lurking in their hair. In the 1950s hair washing certainly did not take place more than once a week as
a rule, thus giving the 'little friends' time to make
themselves well and truly at home. Sixty years on,
the amusing advertisements on television for clear-
ing head lice reveal that the problem is still with us,
but at least nowadays it is recognised that the infes-
tation is not a sign, as was once thought, of a dirty,
neglected child. In the 1950s getting rid of nits was
not thought of as a fun process, as the following
account shows:

Maintaining a clean head can only be done by routine
washing and small tooth combing of the hair, at least
once a week ... The child usually scratches his head
when there is any trace of vermin present. Many
methods of cleaning dirty heads have been used in
the past, the chief one being a compress of carbolic
solution, or a paraffin preparation or sassafras [from
the North American tree; it had various medical
uses]. These are quite unnecessary ... if carelessly
applied may be a danger to the eyes. In treating
dirty heads remember that the child is not the guilty
party, and the approach must be sympathetic and
understanding. The child is sensitive and a compress
labels him to his playmates.

The head tray must be prepared before starting with
a bowl of disinfectant, possibly Dettol, (1 dram to 1

pint of water) a bowl or jar of cotton wool swabs, a receiver for dirty swabs, a Sackers comb [the special metal comb made by Sackers] – Lethane [a pesticide that could prove fatal if ingested or inhaled], a mackintosh cape and derbac soap. [This black and evil-smelling 'soap' was not made from fat as most soaps are but had a strong caustic action. It was said to immobilise the lice, which would die within twenty-four hours. Many mothers treated their children with it as part of the weekly hair-washing routine.]

<u>General Technique.</u> The child should be made as comfortable as possible. Remove outer garments and apply the mackintosh cape – comb and wash the hair with derbac soap. Rinse the hair. After rubbing fairly dry remove the towel but retain the cape. Comb the hair and be careful not to fluff it about. Part the hair into sections, and then with the small tooth comb dipped in disinfectant, comb a few strands of hair, examining the result carefully each time and wiping the comb with a swab. After going all over the hair, burn all swabs. Finish drying the hair and dress it in the usual way unless it is very dirty when it is advisable to apply Lethane or a similar preparation. To do this, make several partings in the hair, apply about five drops to the scalp in a few places and rub all over the scalp. Comb as little as possible to keep the hair tidy and at the end of 10 days – wash and small tooth comb the hair again – when it should be clean.

A.B. Meering, *A Handbook for Nursery Nurses*
(Ballière Tindall & Cox, 1947)

My apologies to any reader who has recalled the horror of this process or had to put it into operation on their children during the 1950s. If it is any consolation my head has itched the whole time I have written this last page! It may not have been the best way to end the subject of bringing up baby in the 1950s, but it does show that in spite of all the progress we have made in the last sixty or more years, mothers are still facing the same problems.

Sources

Books

Liddiard, Mabel, *The Mothercraft Manual* (London: J. &
   A. Churchill Ltd, 1946).
Meering, A.B., *A Handbook for Nursery Nurses* (Ballière,
   Tindall & Cox, 1947).
The *Sunday Express Baby Book*: Prenatal–Six Years
   (Sunday Express, 1950).
Vert Memorial Hospital, *The Baby Book* (Newbourne
   Publications Ltd, 1956).
Your Baby and You (The Nestlé Company).

Magazines

Mother (Odhams Press Ltd), January 1951 and May 1961.
Mother and Baby (Firmins Ltd), 1st edn, January 1956.
Stitchcraft (Condé Nast Ltd), 1951–59.
Woman's Weekly (The Amalgamated Press
   Ltd), April 1958.

Appendices

Significant Events of the 1950s

1950

※
※ February: At the General Election, the Labour
Government returned to power with a majority
of five seats over all other parties.
※ War in Korea.
※ The United States began their hydrogen bomb
programme.

1951

※ The Festival of Britain: 'All through the summer
and all through the land ... will be one act of
national reassessment, and one corporate reaf-

firmation of faith in the nation's future.' (Taken from *The Guide to the South Bank Exhibition*.)

This project was a tremendously optimistic undertaking bearing in mind that it was only six years since the end of the war and the country as a whole was still suffering from acute shortages in practically every area. However, not only did it showcase what British industry could produce, it also brought in foreign visitors and commercial buyers, as well as providing the nation as a whole the opportunity to visit the exhibition and the pleasure gardens that became known as Battersea Fun Fair and the more long-lasting cultural activities at the Festival Hall. Cheap excursion fares allowed people from all over the country the opportunity to visit London and see the exhibition for themselves. Those who could not make the journey were not denied the chance to share in the delight of some of the exhibits: the Guinness clock, for example, toured many seaside resorts.

The Miss World beauty contests began.

Despite the success of the festival, the government itself was in trouble and in October, only eighteen months into their term, Prime Minister Clement Attlee called an election in the hope of winning a more workable majority. The Conservatives were returned with a majority of seventeen and Winston Churchill returned to office for the last time.

1952

February: King George VI died.

The Great London Smog brought the city to a standstill for four days and was responsible for large numbers of deaths from pulmonary-related diseases.

* The passing of the Clean Air Act and the resulting use of smokeless fuel.
* The introduction of the Salk vaccine against polio.

1953

* Disastrous flooding along the east coast in February led to the loss of many lives and the destruction of homes, including those newly erected prefabricated houses. These, being single-storey offered no escape to a higher floor for those trapped in them.
* Charlie Chaplin's last film *Limelight* was showing at the cinema.
* June: Coronation of Queen Elizabeth II complete with the enormous crowds who came to watch it. The event was televised and was responsible for many families deciding to have a TV set in their homes. Throughout the country, street parties, like those which had celebrated VE and VJ Day, again brought communities together. For those without access to television – and it was still limited to certain parts of the country – a full-length colour film of the main events of the day was later shown in cinemas.
* Edmund Hilary and Tensing made history by successfully reaching the summit of Mount Everest.
* DNA was discovered.

1954

* The first atomic submarine was launched.
* A report on cigarette smoking revealed the link with cancer.
* Roger Bannister ran the four-minute mile.

1955

* The Warsaw pact was signed.
* Felt-tip pens were introduced.
* Tests were carried out on fibre optics for mass digital communication.
* Mary Quant opened her boutique in the King's Road, Chelsea.
* Churchill resigned as prime minister through ill health and was succeeded by Anthony Eden.

1956

* The Suez Crisis. The closure of the Suez Canal to British shipping had a serious impact on our trade.
* The Hungarian Revolution.
* IBM created the first hard disk drive.
* Elvis Presley had a hit with *Love me Tender*.

1957

* Anthony Eden resigned as prime minister after criticism of his handling of the Suez Crisis and through ill health.
* *The Cat in the Hat*, by Dr Seuss, was published.
* Proposals were made for the Channel Tunnel.
* Russia sent a Sputnik into space.
* Premium Bonds were introduced.

1958

✳ Lego and Hula Hoops were introduced.

1959

✳ March: Campaign for Nuclear Disarmament held a huge rally in Trafalgar Square.

✳ April: The Cod War with Iceland over fishing rights.

✳ Empire Day renamed Commonwealth Day. In years gone by celebrations had taken place. There was a rhyme that went: 'The twenty-fourth of May is Empire day, if we don't get a holiday, we'll all run away.'

✳ *Juke Box Jury* became a feature of Saturday night TV viewing, particularly aimed at teenagers.

✳ December: first showing on Independent television of *Ivor the Engine* for the younger viewers.

✳ Margaret Thatcher was elected as a Member of Parliament.

Popular Names in the 1950s

Alan, Anthony, Charles, Colin, David, Gary, George, Frank, Ian, James, John, Joseph, Keith, Kenneth, Lawrence, Michael, Paul, Peter, Philip, Raymond, Richard, Robert, Rodney, Ronald, Simon, Stephen, Steven, Terence, William.

Angela, Ann, Barbara, Brenda, Carol, Carolyn, Deborah, Diane, Donna, Elizabeth, Irene, Jacqueline, Jane, Janice, Jennifer, Julie, Karen, Kathleen, Lesley,

Linda, Lynn, Margaret, Marilyn, Mary, Nancy, Pamela, Patricia, Sally, Sandra, Sharon, Shirley, Susan, Valerie.

Popular Advertisements from the 1950s

Baby Foods

✳   Cow & Gate Ltd – 'has achieved a world-wide reputation as the perfect substitute when natural feeding fails, by refusing to compromise between quality and cost.' 'Twelve royal babies to date have been fed on Cow & Gate. Can you do better for your baby?'

✳   Farex – 'From 15 lbs till all 20 milk teeth are through.'

Farley's Rusks.

✳   Heinz – 'Have fun teaching baby to enjoy his food!'

✳   Libby's Strained & Homogenized Vegetables, Fruits & Soups.

✳   Ovaltine Rusks – 'Chuckles – deliciously sweet and crisp make the ideal first solid food for babies.'

✳   Quaker Oats Ltd – 'What's new in the cereal field? The Toasty-Oaty taste of Oat Krunchies.'

✳   Robinson's – 'New High-Protein cereal for when baby starts to play.'

✳   Scott's Baby-cereal twin pack – oat & wheat (alternate the packs).

✳   Trufood – 'When doctors tell you Humanised Trufood is nearest to breast milk they mean not only that it has the vital food elements of pure milk, but has them in proportions practically the same as breast milk. Also – Trufood Strained & Homogenised Spoonfoods in handy, hygienic glass jars from your chemist.'

*　Vitasac – 'Backward babies need Vitasac – Babies improve rapidly on Vitasac because it is readily digested and also eliminates 'wind' … builds up happy active child, regular in habits & enjoying sound sleep.'

Prams etc.

*　Davies – The baby carriage specialist.
*　Marmet (pram) – 'Cool in Summer, Warm in Winter.'
*　Derekot – 'Carry your baby in a folding Derekot.'
*　Karri-Kot – 'Pelso the original folding …'
*　Luxicot.

Washing Powders

*　Johnson's Baby Suds – 'Why you should wash baby's nappies with Baby Suds …'
*　Lux – 'If it's safe in water, it's safe in Lux.'
*　Omo – 'Great Fashion offer! Save 5s 0d on these fluffy white gloves and beret in the softest of soft angora.'
*　Oxydol – 'Washes whiter than bleach.'
*　Persil – 'New whiter Persil washes Whiter! … Coloureds too!'
*　Rinso – 'For whites that are whiter than new.'
*　Tide's In – 'Dirt's Out – 'Yes … all the dirt!'

Food and Drink

*　Bengers.
*　Crosse & Blackwell Soups.
*　Delrosa – rose hip syrup – 'three times as rich in vital Vitamin C.'

* Haliborange.
* Horlicks.
* Hovis bread.
* You'll feel a lot better if you drink more MILK.
* Little Miss Muffet – 'fruit flavoured junkets.'
* Marmite.
* Niagra – blackcurrant drink – 'the nicest way of taking Vitamin C.'
* Ovaltine.
* OXO – 'You <u>can</u> go shopping with a penny!'
* Procea bread.
* Seven Seas cod liver oil.

Remedies and Medicines.

* Aston & Parsons – 'Infants' Powders for teething time.'
* California Syrup of Figs.
* Cannon – 'Modern anit-colic teats for nearest to natural feeding.'
* Cuticura – 'The pure, mildly medicated comfort of Cuticura Talcum.'
* Dentinox – 'Stop teething pains.'
* Dinneford's – 'Doctors and Baby Clinics agree Dinneford's is a most suitable form of magnesia, even for tiny babies.'
* Flowerdells Worm Treatment – 'Dual active tablets – eliminate the worms completely; builds up the body's resistance to further infection, do not cause biliousness or colic, are pleasant to take.'
* Germaloids for piles – 'Is this secret worry necessary?'
  Karsote vapour rub.

* Pineate Honey Cough Syrup – 'Is there a cough in the house?'
* Maw's Teat – 'for bottle-fed babies.'
* Milk of magnesia.
* Raspberry Leaf Tablets – 'For Mother-To-Be – 1. Enable you to enjoy excellent health during your waiting time and 2. Give you a much less painful and much shorter period of labour.'
* Steedman's Powders – 'Happy the baby whose mother knows the benefit of Steedman's Powders, so handy … so easy … so absolutely right for bringing back the smile to baby when he is cross.'
* Virol – 'Growing-up is an energetic business.'
* Wincarnis – 'is wonderful when Housewives are wearied.'
* Woodward's Gripe Water – Keeps baby well and happy.
* Zac – 'Best baby Cream ever used.'

Clothes

* Cherub – socks, underwear, slumberwear.
* Chilprufe for Children – 'Happy as the day … & safe in Chilprufe.'
* Clarks Play-Ups – 'The first steps to confident feet.'
* Jumping Jacks – 'For little feet on the grow.'
* Kamella – 'Guaranteed health garments.'
* Ladybird children's wear.
* Marigold – baby pants – 'super soft fully adjust-able with popper fastenings and waterproof …'
* Marathon – 'Rhovyl one way nappy – Baby's closest friend!'
* Paddi and Paddi-pads – 'no more nappy washing.'

* Punch & Judy socks – 'for the busiest feet in the world.'
* Russelda knitwear – 'my mummy loves Russelda knitwear … with me inside.'
* Start-rite – 'the step ahead sandal-shoes with a fitting for every foot.'

Author's note

Where I have referred to or quoted from any of the above I have acknowledged the material within my text. However, in the sixty years or more since most of the material was first published, many of the original publishers have either ceased trading or been merged into other companies, some of them several times, making the discovery of copyright holders difficult. However, I persevered until I was able to make applications to all concerned for permission to quote specific passages or to use illustrations.

IPC-Media gave permission to quote from *Mother* magazine of January 1951 and May 1961; Bauer Media gave permission to quote from *Mother and Baby* magazine No.1 Vol.1, January 1956, as did the publishers of *Woman's Weekly*.

I have made every effort to contact and secure permission for all sources used. In the case where this has not been achieved the fault is my own, and please contact the publishers in this instance.

All the photographs and items of personal memorabilia herein have been reproduced with the permission of the owners, each of whom has been named and thanked in the Acknowledgements. So, for those kind people who raided the family photograph albums but would rather not now be named, it has been decided that only a descriptive caption should appear with each illustration.

Index

Also by Sheila Hardy

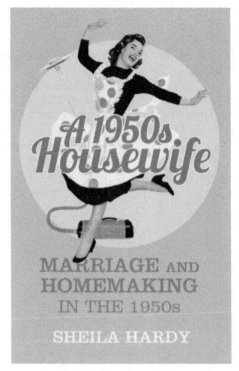

9 780 7509 6414 2

The destination for history
www.thehistorypress.co.uk